ENDORSEMENTS FOR
MISSION ACCOMPLISHED

For anyone planning a missions trip for a team, *Mission Accomplished* by Ron Pratt will help you: 1) have the right mindset; 2) know the right questions to ask; and 3) provide down-to-earth examples for you to adapt. If you are planning a missions trip, you need to read this book.

Dr. J. Melvyn Ming
Leadership Development Resources, LLC
Founding Partner
Executive Director for Pastoral Care & Development
Northwest Ministry Network

Make no mistake, Ron Pratt has written *Mission Accomplished* to addict your heart to a mission mindset. It reads as a one-of-a-kind invitation to a life journey to transform the way you see missions.

His passion is contagious, his message invaluable. He writes an explorers' manual to cut through clichés and send you into the world to reach past culture and circumstances and get to the heart of the people.

A must-read manual for a discipled generation.

Lloyd Zeigler
Director of Master's Commission USA
CEO of MCIN

Ron Pratt's book, *Mission Accomplished*, is a wealth of inspiring and practical material from a man who is doing it on the mission field in Alaska. This captivating book is filled with excellent real-life illustrations.

And there is material I have seen nowhere else, like the chapter on the importance of observing protocol and gifting in Native villages.

Interested in short-term missions for yourself or your church? Reading Ron's book ahead of time can help to make your trip far more effective. I heartily recommend you read *Mission Accomplished*.

L. Alton Garrison
Assistant General Superintendent
Assemblies of God

My family spent 16 years on the field in Southern Africa. During that time we hosted dozens and dozens of teams ... everything from youth groups to a "granny brigade." I wish I would have had this book to give to teams before they came to Africa. What great insights on cross-cultural communication and effectiveness. If this book would have been available then, it would have been required reading before any team, or pastor for that matter, came to do short-term trips.

Now that I am a senior pastor, sending out short- and long-term missionaries, it IS required reading. This book has more practical help than all of the missions books combined that I was required to read before my missions' appointment. If you're doing cross-cultural missions ... you need this.

David Betzer
Lead Pastor
Grace Community Assembly of God
Branson, Missouri

In every generation God releases a voice, one that identifies the obscure and simplifies the complex. With *Mission Accomplished*, Ron Pratt has taken the subject matter of missions, related to the church and the un-churched, and articulated with great accuracy the platitudes, as well as the pitfalls, of building a successful missionary outreach. His insights and understanding are sure to challenge your personal proclivities and awaken your spiritual responsibilities. After reading this book one theme stands out! We are all called to participate in the Great Commission. We are called to invest ourselves in His Kingdom.

Daniel W. Baker
President & CEO
Restoration Ministries

Ron and Yolanda Pratt truly are 21st century missionaries called by God to the Last Frontier to reach the indigenous people of Alaska.

In *Mission Accomplished*, Ron shares practical insights that are Biblical, timeless and cross-culturally relevant that will assist missionaries in fulfilling the Great Commission mandate. His stories are of an Alaskan bush he has personally experienced. They are exciting, thrilling and compelling. He has lived and is living a missional life. He is qualified to speak on the topic of missions and has demonstrated fruitfulness in the Great Land of Alaska. After reading *Mission Accomplished*, you will feel empowered to obey the mandate to "GO into all the world, and share the Good News of Christ!"

Bill Welch
Superintendent
Alaska Ministry Network

It was an absolute joy to read *Mission Accomplished*. Pastor Ron's experiences will be an asset to anyone moving out to the mission field or any other part of ministry. His sense of humor grabs and keeps the reader engaged and makes for an enjoyable reading experience, giving a lighthearted slant to the serious work of reaching the lost for Christ. I highly recommend this book to help "accomplish" your mission.

Otis McCormick
Bishop, District Superintendent
Alaska Church of God in Christ

Ron talks missions. Ron believes in missions. Ron is missions when he is awake; Ron is missions when he sleeps. Ron is missions!

This book is more than a practical how-to guide for planning a successful missions experience. This book is a clarion call for the church to live God's heartbeat for the world. The principles in this book are not just good ideas, they are God's ideas. My dad used to always say, "Son, never buy a Ford from a guy who drives a Chevy." My father taught me a person who lives what they believe can be trusted. The truths in this book come from someone who lives these principles on a daily basis. A person who "drives" what he "sells."

Mark Zweifel
District Youth Director
Alaska Ministry Network

Mission Accomplished is a must-read for everyone wanting to discern God's call in missions, especially if that call takes him or her to the frontiers of Alaska. In its most effective form, the communication of Christ across cultural boundaries is always personal. Without question, much can be learned through interpersonal relationships by carefully considering the contents of this work. Weaving together personal narrative and Biblical insight, *Mission Accomplished* puts forth the clarion call for Christians not to neglect the public proclamation of the Gospel in today's world.

Once you begin reading this book, you won't be able to put it down! You will find this author's "quiet voice" has relevance and immediacy to the challenges in the last frontiers of Alaska. Truth never changes, and it must be packaged culturally and generationally to make it relevant. Author Ron Pratt combines both insight and foresight, perceiving the tendencies common to cross-cultural workers, and is able to pinpoint those meanings for the reader. This work will retain a lasting validity that can be studied and restudied. Pratt's overriding concern is to show that short- and long-term missionary methods are far from being secondary or indifferent matters. Indeed, they are matters of supreme importance. Inviting us to follow in the footsteps of St. Paul in the marketplace of Athens, Ron Pratt calls upon the reader to proclaim Jesus and the Resurrection in the "naked public square" of contemporary Alaskan realities.

Rev John E. Maracle
Mohawk Wolf Clan
Chief/President Native American Fellowship
Assemblies of God Executive Presbyter Ethnic Fellowships

The terms "authenticity" and "relevance" are well-worn in recent days but are certainly hugely important when considering the operation and claims of 21st century ministry endeavors. It is my delight to affirm Ron Pratt and TGM (This Generation Ministries) as "poster children" for both of these concepts! Having personally spent a year in Alaska granted me the privilege of knowing Ron, his family, his team and his ministry from a special vantage point.

When reading the book, *Mission Accomplished*, you enter their world and are allowed the incredible opportunity of experiencing the passion, joys and victories, as well as the uncertainties and struggles brought to life through the Kingdom exploits of true-to-life Alaska missions. This book grants the reader great insights into missions' ministry in the rugged environs of Northern Alaska, but the principles contained therein also have tremendous value for trans-contextual application. So fasten your seatbelt, prepare your heart and mind to be challenged and get ready for an incredible journey as you travel into the pages of this great adventure!

Sam Hemby, Ph.D.
Professor and Director
CCMR Graduate Programs
Southeastern University
Lakeland, Florida

I have had the privilege to be a part of Ron Pratt's ministry since I was a teenager, starting with having him as a youth pastor from 2000 to 2003. Between my youth group experience and the following three years as a student of the Master's Commission program, which Pratt directed, I have been molded and shaped into the man of God that I am today.

Into this book, *Mission Accomplished: The Secrets of Successful Missions*, Ron Pratt pours much of the teaching and experience of his many years of successful ministry. I am honored to have been a part of many of the stories within the chapters of this "Missions Manual." It is through the direction, mentorship and investment of time, prayer, pain and tears of Ron Pratt that my wife and I have come to be lead pastors of Fort Yukon Assembly of God since 2006.

I attribute much of our success and longevity in this remote Yukon Flats village to the godly habits, skills and behaviors instilled into me throughout the years that were spent under Ron Pratt's ministry and teaching. Many of these teachings can be found within the pages of *Mission Accomplished.*

My hope is that this book will be a helpful tool for local church leaders to bring their missions programs and outreach endeavors to the next level of excellence and fruitfulness, to the glory of God. I believe so strongly in the concepts and teachings in this book that I have made this book required reading for churches and individuals who fly up to the Yukon Flats to assist us in ministry through mission teams. I hope and pray that God speaks to you, inspires you and encourages you through this book.

Pastor Jeremiah Niemuth
Assembly of God U.S. Missionary
to the Yukon Flats Region of Alaska
Lead Pastor
Fort Yukon Assembly of God

MISSION ACCOMPLISHED

The Secrets of Successful Missions

RON PRATT

Dedication

This book reflects decades of ministry, hardships, challenges, steps of faith and the wonderful joys of success. These difficulties were not conquered alone, nor were the many victories achieved on my own. It is with the deepest of love and adoration, therefore, that I dedicate *Mission Accomplished* to my partner in life and ministry, my loving wife, Yolanda Marie Pratt.

Yolanda, you kept me focused during times of distraction. You endured my nocturnal writing habits, and you kept me covered in prayer when I most needed it. Thank you for your love, dedication, faithfulness and priceless support.

Your loving Papa Bear

Ron and Yolanda Pratt

Table of Contents

FOREWORD
by Ken Horn

It was seven years ago that I first boarded a small boat in an Alaskan village and watched Ron Pratt navigate the mighty Yukon River to the place where he and his ministry team set up camp for the night.

Pratt and his team of 15 students and staff were in the midst of their fifth annual outreach on the river system. Since then the ministry has grown, and in 2012, I returned to see the top-drawer wilderness camp that has emerged from that earlier ministry to reach at-risk Native youth from remote areas.

Pratt, an Assemblies of God missionary evangelist, founded and directs *This Generation Ministries* (TGM) and Camp Nahshii.

Alaska is known as "The Last Frontier." The Aleuts called it Alyeska, the Great Land. And great it is — consisting of 586,000 square miles. Though it is sparsely populated, Alaska still contains some 731,500 inhabitants, and nearly everywhere in the state there is need for more of the Gospel of Jesus Christ. Alaska is still a mission field — a spiritual frontier.

Larger cities on the "road system" are more modern and the lifestyles more familiar to that in the lower 48 states. The more remote villages have not been untouched by civilization, but they still bear many of the marks of the primitive heritage of the Native people groups. It is to this difficult frontier that Ron Pratt has been called. And the mighty Yukon has become the gateway to his effective ministry.

The Yukon River is one of the granddaddies of the world's waterways. From its headwaters in Canada, it flows some 1,980 miles through the Yukon Territory and central Alaska before ending, at its mouth in the Bering Sea, at the village of St. Michael.

Yukon is a Gwich'in Athabascan word meaning a great, wide river. And that it is.

It is miles wide in some places. But the massive waters flow over frequently shallow areas as well, resulting in a changing topography — islands appearing one year, only to be swallowed up the next. Those who navigate these waters must be experienced, cautious and prepared.

It was summer at Camp Nahshii, on the shores of a Yukon River tributary, when I observed an interchange that punctuated the importance of this ministry to me. Pratt sat at a sturdy, rough-hewn, camp-made picnic table facing a 14-year-old boy from a small village on the Yukon. A few short years before, this boy had first come to Camp Nahshii, broken in spirit and scarred by a tragic family life.

This day would mark a major milestone in his life journey. Pratt had selected the boy to be considered for the young leaders program. Pratt has a passion not only to see lives like this one turned around by God, but also to empower the young villagers and develop the next generation to lead. It's the way many of his current leaders began their ministries.

Now this boy wants to make a difference, and he feels called to the ministry. Pratt believes the boy is ready for the next step. It is the way of this ministry — not just saving souls, but building lives.

Nahshii means "healing" in the language of the Gwich'in Athabascans, the dominant people group in this area of Eastern Alaska along the upper Yukon River. And it is indeed more than a word.

Ron Pratt and his wife, Yolanda, were called to Alaska in 1998. With a burden for the youth of Alaska, Pratt eventually found a fertile field for the Gospel in the remote villages of the state. Pratt's first village outreach was to an Eskimo village in the summer of 1999.

"It just broke my heart for the Native people," he told me. "It put a fire in me to create and train teams and raise up people to minister in the villages."

He's been doing that ever since. It was 2003 when he took the first of his teams to minister on the Yukon River, putting in at Circle, a small village some 90 miles from Fort Yukon, and ministering in villages and fish camps. It is a joy to see how the ministry has evolved and grown since then.

Since I have seen this ministry up close and personal, I was thrilled to hear that Ron was writing a book. And I felt privileged when asked to write this foreword.

Mission Accomplished: The Secrets of Successful Missions is a unique book, written by one whose credentials have been proven on the mission field. Because of the author's experience, the book is supremely practical. Pratt has lived the adventure, struggled through the trials, suffered the defeats and reaped the harvest of perseverance.

Pratt makes that valuable experience available to the reader. His ministry story is woven into a Biblical discussion and practical handbook of missions. The book's approach is replete with examples. Fascinating narratives build a visible structure for the teaching in the book, helping readers to see with the mind's eye rather than simply comprehending concepts.

And nothing is candy-coated.

The challenges of ministry in The Last Frontier are immense … and costly. But, as Pratt says in the book: "You can't afford to invest into missions? Really? Actually, you can't afford not to!"

I agree.

In the pages that follow, you will find an adventure story grounded in Biblical doctrine and augmented by practical direction. The information on understanding and reaching other cultures is, in itself, a wealth of ministry treasure.

Honor is an important concept to Pratt — honoring the leaders and honoring the customs of the people have helped to open doors for his ministry. And it has helped him develop a strong ministry model, creating structure with flexibility, a balance that can be difficult to maintain.

The author trumpets the value of short-term (and

mid-term) missions, if they are done right. The "one-night stand" style of missions hurts all parties involved, he says. That makes the need for missionaries to "build lasting relationships" all the more important.

His team has become adept at integrating new personnel into their somewhat difficult ministry. Should you come, you will work hard, but he and his team have sanded down all the rough edges.

The book is humorous. In the story of the unwanted visitor (now known as the "Prayer Bear") that interrupted a prayer time, for example, Pratt draws some interesting lessons from the incident.

It is also serious. That same bear destroyed their new Cabela's tent, became aggressive and Pratt was forced to shoot it. Pratt dressed it with the help of a tribal elder. I met up with the group for the first time shortly after this and shared in a meal of bear meat.

TGM is not about just holding a successful camp or even transforming the lives of Native teens. It is about making an impact so deep it will be felt in communities up and down the remote Yukon River.

That's exactly what they are doing — and this is their story.

Ken Horn
Author and Editor
Pentecostal Evangel
Official Magazine of the Assemblies of God

Introduction
Planning a Successful
Missions Outreach

They said they were prepared and seasoned. They had practiced skits, and a few on the team had assisted with a Vacation Bible School or two. Some were finishing up their pastoral ministry studies. Others, from the same Bible college, were still seeking the Lord for direction. But in every case, their program was rehearsed and their flexibility minimal. "Here is what we do; we need to work within these parameters." That was the mentality.

Without any regard to the needs of the community, the style of learning of its people group or the protocols of the culture, we followers of Jesus often use our cookie cutter methods when implementing missions in the field. We expect others to embrace and respond to our approach because we are comfortable with it. When we find resistance or failure, we have a tendency to blame the people or the devil, when in all reality we simply used the wrong methods, wrong approach and came in like superheroes posturing the wrong attitude. "This worked at the last place" is a common assumption that sets a team up for failure, much like it did for our Bible college team.

In sports, there are "acceptable losses," and we understand that mindset: You win some, and you lose some. Eventually, hopefully, you start winning more than you lose. In missions, there should never be any acceptable losses! We can't afford to *not* be successful in freeing the captives!

The Spirit of the Lord is upon me, because He anointed me to preach the Gospel to the poor. He has sent me to proclaim release to the captives, and recovery of sight to the blind, to set free those who are oppressed (Luke 4:18).

This is life or death! A commission given as a command, a mandate that should literally become the most exciting life mission we ever pursue. Whether we are going to the mission field, or we are sending others, it is our wonderful privilege to reach the lost with the best news they will ever hear.

The hope of this book is to be a manual for missions' success. Learning from my many mistakes, failures, triumphs and missions' successes, my prayer is that you will be encouraged, challenged and released to find God's pleasure through the practical, as well as the supernatural. May the favor of Father God anoint your efforts in focused mission living, leaving you with these words to express each mission's effort: *Mission Accomplished.*

Ronald D. Pratt

Chapter One
Missions Defined

From [Christ] the whole body, joined and held together by every supporting ligament, grows and builds itself up in love, as each part does its work. (Ephesians 4:16)

Creative Desperation

Just getting to the river was a great adventure, since much of the landscape was in flames along this 170-mile stretch of road. What should have been a five-hour drive lasted more than 12 hours. The mass of interior land had been overtaken by wildfires.

I, along with most of the team, was exhausted, and I wanted to get this missions trip underway. After several long days of prep, no one on the team had rested adequately, and many of us had pulled some all-nighters. On the way out of town, we encountered more than the usual exit traffic as people headed away from the burning hills we were now heading into. But we were determined.

We had a mandate! We had a schedule to keep! We continued to convoy across gravel, dirt and sometimes muddy road with our sights set on the Yukon River. It's amazing just how far you can travel these back roads while riding on a rim with no tire. What, no spare tire for the boat trailer? We were on a tight budget and even tighter schedule. Finding a spare for that old borrowed trailer just had not been a priority. We covered more than 50 miles until the rim finally deteriorated down to a red-hot axle hub.

What seemed like a week of camping on the riverbank was actually only three days. My team of 15 had been waiting for our third boat and boat captain to arrive to help distribute the bulk and overall weight of our people and gear for our trek down the Yukon River. With a three-week supply of food, fuel, camping gear and ministry supplies, we were in great need of the extra boat. Being more than 100 miles from any cell phone connection and having only one pay phone in the small village that was our embarkation point made communication a bit challenging.

On the third day, I managed to contact the boat captain, only to find out that the forest fires had closed off any access from him to us in this village. The bottom line: The third boat was not coming, and with the road closures, turning this ministry team back was simply not an option.

Many elders and some family had evacuated the village while the roads were still open, and the state forest service had flown in firefighters to the village in case the fires got too close to any homes or structures. Even with a smaller population in this village, there was plenty of ministry work taking place around us, however, because we had become the "happening" entertainment for the locals. But as much as we wanted to continue to minister there, we had villages downriver that were waiting on our arrival. A local Native man that I had met the first day we arrived suggested we build a raft for all of our supplies. He also volunteered his time and experience to help build it. With no better options at the time, I agreed.

About 20 miles upriver, we found a location where we could successfully harvest trees. The plan was to find large spruce trees, preferably ones that were leaning toward the water. After felling several big trees, we dragged them downriver and begin our raft construction. Building a log raft to haul extra gear or supplies was a fairly common practice in this Native community. As we secured logs together, it came to my attention that we had never navigated such a large, awkward object on the Yukon River before. The raft idea was now appearing to look dysfunctional and dangerous at best. Who agreed to this silly idea, anyway? Oh, that would be me. The locals were entertained by our sloppy building, and when I abandoned this doomed plan, they were pleased with our donation of logs.

As it turned out, during that waiting period, we had

gone through enough food and supplies that we could load up the two boats that we had and head downriver. We really had no other option. Due to the growing forest fires, the only road out of town was still closed, leaving us with our backs to the river and an inferno that was rapidly approaching our location.

Challenges come with any missions trip. Many of these difficulties are generated by the culture and circumstances around you. Some of them, however, are self-induced from a lack of planning. This missions venture, like so many, had some of both.

Each day the boats became lighter, and we became a little smarter. We kept our heads and hearts in the game. We ran our race the best we could, and God blessed us with open doors and a wonderful ministry. You learn to love people, serve and do your best. Some missions go better than others, but you keep going because seeing the smiles on those kids' faces is worth all the cost, all the sacrifice and all the struggle. Witnessing the healing hand of Father God touch the hearts of the hurting is what keeps us going. It's the fruit of our labor, a labor we are mandated to do.

I sure wish I could call "do-overs!" for many of my early missions work, but it's best to learn from the past and make method changes for the future. It sure didn't take long to figure out that there is no such thing as a "missions template" to follow. Missions come in such a plethora of forms and different focuses that the needed methods must be flexible. You simply can't say, "This is how you do a missions trip." Neither can you put missionary work or missions outreach in a box and label it.

ॐॐॐ

It was the mid-'80s in California, and if you lived near the West Coast, a missions trip to Mexico was in order. In those days, it was quite economical to travel south over the border and relatively safe, if traveling in a group. The church and pastor we found to support were conveniently located only a few hours over the border. In just a one-day drive, we had arrived and were unpacking the vehicles.

The ministry we did was diverse, yet predictable. Like clockwork, the ministry teams would hit the ground running, work hard, minister to people with an excitement and enjoy the cultural side attractions. Did I mention shopping? The exchange rate was amazing in those days. Well, if you lived north of the Mexican border, it was. I recall hearing those who were seasoned in Mexico mission work speak of their great deals from past trips and of the many potential future shopping locations, if the team leader plans the next trip a little better. "Hopefully, we will get plenty of down time, and some wanted shopping will be had by all!" was often the sentiment.

I must admit, I personally enjoyed negotiating an item down to a fraction of the price tag. I remember walking out of a little shop several times, each time sending the merchant yelling for me to return, as he would have a "new reduction" for my liking. This aggressive bartering method is common outside the walls of our retail culture in the States. When I first asked about a dress for my wife, it was a firm "$95 American dollars." When I walked away with that dress in a brown paper bag, it had cost me $14. The local missionary said to me, "I would have gotten him down to $10, and he still would have made 100 percent profit."

Like many others, I found myself returning home with more conversation focused on the shopping than the ministry work. Shopping can be a great cultural experience and often a real necessity. So we always plan a local stop or two for our mission teams. These little detours can be a great breather from hectic outreach schedules and a great chance to bring home a few gifts. The danger is when these detours become the passion of the heart or the underlying trip agenda of a team member.

When complacency taints the mission, the original purpose can be diluted. The "routine" of missions has the potential of degrading our purpose and diverting our passion if we don't maintain the vision that brought us there in the first place.

Missions Defined

What is "missions"? This seems like a silly question to ask, but I believe that most Christians, and many ministers, have a distorted view of what a mission is and what it is not. I recall many missionaries coming to our church when I was a kid. Looking back, it seemed to me that they were all from Africa. I grew up correlating these two words — *missions* always meant *Africa* to me. For many people, the word *missionary* is synonymous with *foreign*. We have somehow come to think that all missionary work is done overseas, far from our current homeland. Although much missionary work does take place in a foreign or faraway country, there is equally important missionary work happening right in our backyards.

New word, old concept: The word "missionary" is first found in print in 1815. You won't find this word in the pages of the Bible, but its Biblical mandate is obvious. The word missionary is said to have derived from the Neo-Latin word "missionaries," which came into use around 1635-45 AD.

Here is the Webster dictionary definition of "missionary":

1. Person sent by a church into an area to carry on evangelism or other activities, as educational or hospital work.
2. Person strongly in favor of a program, set of principles, etc., who attempts to persuade or convert others.
3. Person who is sent on a <u>mission</u> (adjective).
4. Pertaining to or connected with religious <u>missions</u>.
5. Engaged in such a <u>mission</u> or devoted to work connected with <u>missions</u>.

6. Reflecting or prompted by the desire to persuade or convert others; the missionary efforts of political fanatics.
7. Characteristic of a missionary.

I believe number three sums it up: "person who is sent on a mission." That's us! The believers! All followers of Christ have the same mission, and it's found deep within our spiritual DNA. All we need to do is tap into that DNA and begin implementing our God-given abilities to do that mission.

Six-Fold Ministry?

Some speak of the "missionary" as if this were a missing sixth finger. Let me explain.

It was He who gave some to be apostles, some to be prophets, some to be evangelists, and some to be pastors and teachers, to prepare God's people for works of <u>service</u>, so that the body of Christ may be built up until we all reach unity in the faith and in the knowledge of the Son of God and become mature, attaining to the whole measure of the fullness of Christ. From Him the whole body, joined and held together by every supporting ligament, grows and builds itself up in love, as each part does its work (Ephesians 4:11-13, 16, emphasis added).

We see here the framework of the five-fold ministry. I propose to you that the office of "missionary" is not listed in verse 11 because all five offices are there to *empower* our "*mission*!" I believe "missionary" is an office that fully embodies the five-fold ministry. It's not the missing sixth finger. It actually encompasses and foundationally saturates all five offices of ministry. The missionary does not stand alone. The work and purpose of missions is found within the very grip of this hand.

Furthermore, "missionary" is not a word tied to a distant country. The missionary is simply this: "a person who aids, does religious work." We know that the word "missionary" comes from the word "mission." A missionary is simply a person who is pursuing or carrying out a given mission. All followers of Christ have the same foundational "mission" — a mission to go!

Building Missions Mindset

We all have a missions' mindset. It is found in how we see the world and how we see our place in it. The true missionary mind understands that this "thing" called missions is not intended for a select few but for all believers. Maybe you are a welder. The missionary mind says, "I'm a missionary, but I weld for a living." The school teacher says, "I'm a missionary, but I teach to support my mission." Are you a musician? Then live as a "musicianary."

The Great Commission is Our Mission

16 Then the eleven disciples went to Galilee, to the mountain where Jesus had told them to go. 17 When they saw Him, they worshiped Him; but some doubted. 18 Then Jesus came to them and said, "All authority in heaven and on earth has been given to me. [19] Therefore **go** and make disciples of all nations, baptizing them in the name of the Father and of the Son and of the Holy Spirit, [20] and teaching them to obey everything I have commanded you. And surely I am with you always, to the very end of the age" (Matthew 28:16-20).

Webster's dictionary defines "commission" as:

- the authority to perform a task or certain duties
- an instruction, command or duty given to a person or group of people
- a group of people officially charged with a particular function

Jesus' words above were not intended to be *the great suggestion*. It's literally our "commission" to do our kingdom portion. Jesus has an opinion on this. He said, in John 14:15, *If you love Me, keep My commands*. We don't have the luxury of verbally proclaiming our love for Jesus and then making a choice to do our own thing.

As seen in Matthew 28, the "whole body" is called to missions! The "GO" does not have an age limit — it's directed to every follower of Christ. So, getting out there and doing it must be a personal and collective commission that is seen throughout our tenacious and obedient life.

This great mandate is not simply for the select few. It's a privilege intended for ALL followers of Jesus! So, who are the missionaries? Simply put, WE are! When you and I look in the mirror, we are getting an excellent view of what a missionary looks like. The source of our income has no bearing on our life purpose. We are called, we are commissioned and we are anointed to do this heavenly work of the missionary!

Your mirror reveals the look of a missionary.

As we pursue this thing called missions, we find it has much diversity. Whether it looks like home missions, local missions or foreign missions, it is all missions. Short-term or long-term, the duration does not qualify or disqualify mission work. We simply need to stay busy on our mission.

Before we look at the different durations and benefits of missions, let me clarify what the *office* of missions looks like. One of the misnomers in missions work is that preaching has a greater value over the other aspects of missions. The idea that all "non-preaching" departments of a mission program are somehow "lower" in position and "lesser" in kingdom value than preaching has been propagated from our pulpits for far too long. We have believers who warm the pews of our churches who are convinced that they have no place in missions. They have bought into the idea that Matthew 28 is somehow reserved for the clergy select. Since they don't preach, they suppose there is no place for them in the mission field. The cumulative effect of this missions misconception continues to raise its ugly head in everyday mission planning and work.

Unfortunately, it's common for a church or ministry program leader to ask me if he or she could be involved in some "real ministry," such as preaching the Word. I can't say I always respond to this with grace as it stirs up in me, shall we say, some "holy frustration."

A ministry couple from a large church spent a few days at one of our summer camps in Alaska. Having a pastor, missions director or representative visit one of our ministry locations for a few days is not uncommon. We encourage leaders who are considering missions in Alaska to make a lead trip first. After a few days with us, this couple began to share their future ministry plans and intentions. Like many before and since, they made the statement: "I know you are in need of work teams, but we are more interested in doing real ministry."

Real ministry?!

I did understand what these missionary leaders were asking, just as you may have. But the frustrating part is what they may not know. The mindset they displayed is keeping "missions teams" small and pushing away some very valuable participants. It's this kind of thinking that propagates a clergy/laity relationship (a concept not promoted in the Word) that keeps the follower of Jesus intimidated to answer the "Go" and keeps them warming the pews back home, while those called to preach respond and "Go do something."

The current church culture is clothed in a Western mindset that keeps the average believer thinking he or she simply can't do the "real" work of ministry. Not everyone is called, gifted and anointed to fulfill the public preaching role. But every believer is called to play a part in missions.

Plant and Water

Two different jobs, but with the same reward. Let's take a look at this letter written to the church.

⁸The man who plants and the man who waters have one purpose, and each will be rewarded according to his own labor. ⁹For we are God's fellow workers; you are God's field, God's building (1 Corinthians 3:8-9).

This passage clearly states that we should not communicate levels of worth when it comes to ministry. Yes, the preaching of the Word is majorly important. But I believe all ministries should help foster a climate for successful discipleship.

Whether it's promotions, media, transportation, lodging, hospitality or construction of facilities to preach in, we bottleneck the forward movement of ministry if we teach the body that these areas of involvement are not really ministry.

Whenever I preach from a stage, I recognize that someone built it. When I enter a building of any size that is being used for ministry, I recognize that someone ministered with his or her talents, resources, sweat, tears and heart into building that facility. I see that as "real ministry." Our ministry is driven by our missions calling. Every aspect of this collective kingdom work is missions!

On Target

Think of missions as a target and discipleship as the bull's eye. The first outer ring is very close to the bull's eye (discipleship), and each ring gets just a little farther away.

Each ring is very important and holds a value to the target. And even the last outer ring is necessary for calibration. You see, without the outer rings, you would have difficulty assessing the distance, size and accuracy when shooting for the bull's eye.

We have a human tendency to compare each ring (placement or position) to each other. But if you step back and take a wide-angle view of things, we are actually all on the same page.

So what should we absorb from these two verses? Those who build and those who resource the mission receive:

- the same *blessings*
- the same *reward*
- the same *inheritance*

It really doesn't matter who you are, what title you have or what position you hold in the church. It only matters that your "body part" is actively working in obedience to the Lord. As we read in Ephesians 4:16: *From whom the whole body, being fitted and held together by what every joint supplies, **according to the proper working of each individual part**, causes the growth of the body for the building up of itself in love.*

We are all members of "one" body, the body of Christ. We each serve a strategically valuable part. Our function may be different, but our mission mandate is the same.

For through the grace given to me I say to everyone

among you not to think more highly of himself than he ought to think; but to think so as to have sound judgment, as God has allotted to each a measure of faith. ⁴For just as we have many members in one body and all the members do not have the same function, ⁵so we, who are many, are one body in Christ, and individually members one of another. ⁶Since we have gifts that differ according to the grace given to us, each of us is to exercise them accordingly: if prophecy, according to the proportion of his faith; ⁷if service, in his serving; or he who teaches, in his teaching; ⁸or he who exhorts, in his exhortation; he who gives, with liberality; he who leads, with diligence; he who shows mercy, with cheerfulness (Romans 12:3-8).

Yes, we are one body, but verse 6 reminds us that our gifts for this mission are different:

"Since we have gifts that differ according to the grace given to us, *each of us is to exercise them accordingly.*"

Exercise them accordingly? Yes, we need to apply some physical activity to those gifts and abilities we were given. Those gifts and talents were created and lavished on us, not so we could look cool or sit around being gifted, but so we would use them for kingdom building.

Keeping our gifts hidden and to ourselves is an injustice to the lost and a detriment to our personal growth. Selfishness has never been, nor will it ever be, rewarded with blessing. Withholding our gifts and talents from being employed in our mandated mission is the most selfish thing we could do as a follower of Christ.

In the "Parable of the Talents," found in Matthew

25:14-30, we see a warning that should serve as motivation to invest the talents given to us. We also see a wonderful principle of heaven: If we faithfully use our talents and abilities for their intended kingdom purpose (missions), God will increase our talents.

Many are fearful to step out and be used in ministry because of potential failure. Being used by God has risks. Going on a missions trip has risks. (Just ask anyone who has traveled with me!) Serving Jesus has risks.

Anytime we step out in obedience to the voice and direction of God, we become a bigger target for the enemy, and the risk greatly increases. The bigger the threat we become, the bigger target we become. Anyone can respond out of fear and "hide the talent" that was given. This is exactly what the enemy wants us to do. He knows that when we implement our gifts into kingdom work, he loses ground. He also understands full well that the principles of heaven will supernaturally cause increase in our lives, increasing our weaponry against him.

The increased risks are directly correlated to our level of obedience. Yes, the more we invest our life into our mission, the more we step out of comfort and into the life of faith. But with that same level of personal risk comes supernatural blessing! The servant who hid his talent was punished, but the servant who took a risk and invested his talents was given more.

Mission Way of Thinking

Cultivating a "mission way of thinking" might take some time, since we have been subjected to a lifetime of "Western church" culture, a culture that often paints a picture of separating lines in ministry.

Before we can step out into a lifestyle of mission living, we first need to allow a transformation of our thoughts and beliefs to take place. As this paradigm shift begins on the inside, walking in a mission lifestyle will become the norm. Cultivating a mission mindset will transform lives, beginning with your own.

There are no spiritual loopholes that exclude us from Matthew 28. Nor is there a position earned with a La-Z-Boy chair provided. You and I are commissioned to go! And a great reward will follow those who actively join in this missionary work called the "Great Commission." The body of Christ will successfully reach a hurting world as each part does its work.

Chapter Two
Missions Diversity

How will they preach unless they are sent? Just as it is written, "How beautiful are the feet of those who bring good news of good things!" (Romans 10:15)

Off the Road

It was a very familiar drive, about three hours each way, which was not too bad a trip to reach an Alaskan village. We had managed our way there without any trouble. But during those three days in the village, the snow had dumped on the mountaintops, making our drive home a bit challenging. With the temperature warming up, the roads were bound to be slick. Navigating a snowy backwoods road in the dark of night is always a little scary, and the task of staying on the road can be tough when you can't see the road.

Mission Accomplished

After successfully getting through the snowdrifts and over the pass, I was sure that we were through the worst of it. While slowing down for an upcoming junction in the road, I quickly became aware that the brakes were not earning their keep. The ground was covered in a sheet of ice, and no traction could be found.

Then our small mission team slid across the road in a large pickup truck! Over the snowy embankment, with the nose pointed straight for the ledge, downward we went. Fortunately, the thick, freshly fallen snow built up under the front of the truck and brought us to a stop.

Wow, there we were, after midnight, out of view of the road, over the hill, and looking down through the front windshield. The truck had not been damaged, but we were packed very deep in the snow. I shifted it into four-wheel drive and then reverse, but that was just digging us deeper into the hill. Even opening the truck doors was difficult because the snow had us packed in tight. To our advantage, the temperature had warmed up to -10 degrees, making it much more bearable to be outside as we attempted to wave down traffic.

Traffic may not be the right word for what we were waiting for. This was the "haul road," a road system that is mostly traveled by big rigs taking the long trek to Prudhoe Bay and back. Being on this remote stretch of road on a weekend, especially after midnight, the traffic would be slim at best.

As expected, we waited about 30 minutes before we saw the massive lights of a big rig heading north. We crawled out of the truck and climbed up the hill to wave this trucker down.

It took him quite a distance to come to a complete stop, but he did. He was kind enough to run some long chains down the hill and attempted to pull us out. It didn't take long to see that his 18-wheeler, with an empty trailer, was only spinning out on the ice. So, he got on the radio and spoke to a trucker heading south with a full load. The loaded rig had the weight to do the job. The southbound trucker stopped, chained up his drive tires and pulled that F350 up the hill like it was a scooter. We showed our appreciation, knowing that the nearest towing service was more than 100 miles away and would have cost us in excess of $1,500 just to get towed back onto the road.

It was around 2 a.m. when we were finally free to complete our journey. After digging out the snow, packed tight in every crevasse of the frame, we finally headed south to get home. The next month, we headed up that same road again. Ministry has its costs and sometimes danger, and it rarely comes in a comfortable package.

Missions Diversity

When I hear the words "missionary work," so many different scenarios flash through my mind. You can find several cultures within a culture, right in your own city, town or region.

Here, in Alaska, we have about 230 federally recognized Alaskan Native tribes. Many of these tribes have multiple villages which have cultivated their own distinct culture, even within their tribe. Upon further inspection, we often find that there is evidence of unique cultural separation within a single village.

I'm sure this concept is not new to you. You understand that there is great diversity in mission work. My focus, in this segment, is to prepare you, mentally and spiritually, for the unique culture that you are about to enter. It is a culture that you must understand in order to have the wisdom to reach the people who live by that culture.

You can't bring transformation to what you are following.

One of the mistakes we see in mission work is an over-emphasis on a given culture. Culture should be respected and recognized but not necessarily supported and embraced. I believe every culture has elements that should be revived and honored, and other elements that should be discarded and forgotten. We should be ready to speak to and through the culture without becoming influenced by it.

Hudson Taylor was a missionary to China who stood out like a sore thumb. His unique approach gave him a voice that others had spent years attempting to gain. Realizing that the traditional missionary model was failing to reach the Chinese culture, Hudson decided to honor their culture by adapting to their dress code.

Hudson spent 52 years on the Chinese mission field (1853 to 1905). In those decades of ministry, he can be remembered for one unique thing — he grew out a long ponytail, dyed it black and shaved the rest of his head, as was the relevant custom of the Chinese culture in those days. That is how the men dressed, and that is who he wanted to reach.

However, this missionary did not embrace every part of the Chinese culture. No, I'm not dissing the Chinese. I absolutely love them. After all, they gave us the noodle and gunpowder! But Hudson knew that you can't change the direction of something you are following. You must find a place to lead it.

Allow me to note here that the hairstyle Hudson adopted was not born out of rebellion. It was not a style designed by a smaller sect of people trying to make a statement against a system.

It was actually the honorable style of the day, a look that symbolized honor, prestige and unity. He joined this symbol of unity so that he could give a voice to the Gospel of Jesus that would be heard.

Having the wisdom to know what to support and what not to support is vital to the success of any mission. The missionary work of Hudson Taylor became very effective as the Chinese people accepted him and his Gospel. Although the people he met had not heard of Jesus prior to meeting Hudson, they began to trust him and his message.

It becomes dangerous when a missionary accepts, embraces and promotes *all* areas of a given culture. We never see Jesus going into a city or region with the intent to promote or even restore a culture. He actually spoke against the traditions of man and offered a new covenant to follow. Everything he did caused people to follow Him and either adapt to Jesus' culture or reject it.

It is misleading when we try to "add Jesus" to any culture. Those who agree to "accept Jesus into their lifestyle" will always look at Jesus as an addendum to their beliefs and view Him as equal to or lesser than their ancient beliefs and traditions.

I've even heard ministers say, "Why don't you give Jesus a try?" They have great intentions, I'm sure, but we don't "try out" our Savior any more than you would try out a lifeguard while gasping for your last breath. When we take up our cross, we don't give Jesus a chance. He gives us one.

Culture should always be understood, but not always followed.

[16] Now while Paul was waiting for them at Athens, his spirit was being provoked within him as he was observing the city full of idols. [17] So he was reasoning in the synagogue with the Jews and the God-fearing Gentiles, and in the market place every day with those who happened to be present. [18] And also some of the Epicurean and Stoic philosophers were conversing with him. Some were saying, "What would this idle babbler wish to say?" Others, "He seems to be a proclaimer of strange deities,"— because he was preaching Jesus and the resurrection. [19] And they took him and brought him to the Areopagus, saying, "May we know what this new teaching is which you are proclaiming? [20] For you are bringing some strange

things to our ears; so we want to know what these things mean." [21] (Now all the Athenians and the strangers visiting there used to spend their time in nothing other than telling or hearing something new.)

[22] So Paul stood in the midst of the Areopagus and said, "Men of Athens, I observe that you are very religious in all respects. [23] For while I was passing through and examining the objects of your worship, I also found an altar with this inscription, 'TO AN UNKNOWN GOD.' Therefore what you worship in ignorance, this I proclaim to you. [24] The God who made the world and all things in it, since He is Lord of heaven and earth, does not dwell in temples made with hands; [25] nor is He served by human hands, as though He needed anything, since He Himself gives to all people life and breath and all things; [26] and He made from one man every nation of mankind to live on all the face of the earth, having determined their appointed times and the boundaries of their habitation, [27] that they would seek God, if perhaps they might grope for Him and find Him, though He is not far from each one of us; [28] for in Him we live and move and exist, as even some of your own poets have said, 'For we also are His children.' [29] Being then the children of God, we ought not to think that the Divine Nature is like gold or silver or stone, an image formed by the art and thought of man. [30] Therefore having overlooked the times of ignorance, God is now declaring to men that all people everywhere should repent, [31] because He has fixed a day in which He will judge the world in righteousness through a Man whom He has appointed,

having furnished proof to all men by raising Him from the dead."

[32] Now when they heard of the resurrection of the dead, some began to sneer, but others said, "We shall hear you again concerning this." [33] So Paul went out of their midst. [34] But some men joined him and believed, among whom also were Dionysius the Areopagite and a woman named Damaris and others with them (Acts 17:16-34).

We see in this scriptural account that the Apostle Paul was aware of the culture and worked within that culture to influence the people around him. Here in Alaska, we work within the local culture and its protocols (more on protocol in Chapter Eight) to earn a voice into the lives of that people group. There are many aspects of the Native Alaskan culture that we promote, observe and even reintroduce. For example: processing fish, working a trap line, woodwork, food preparation and arctic survival are overall healthy traditions.

However, we stand against any elements of culture which go against the teachings of the Word of God. Some of these are new traditions, added to Native Alaskan culture recently, such as alcoholism and drug abuse. And some are ancient traditions, like worship of the dead, superstitions, divination and shamanism.

sha·man (thefreedictionary.com)

A member of certain tribal societies who acts as a medium between the visible world and an invisible spirit world and who practices magic or sorcery for purposes of healing, divination and control over natural events.

While the worldly view of culture is all-inviting and supportive of *every* aspect of a culture, the missionary view must draw a defined line in the sand and never tolerate works of the enemy.

¹I solemnly charge you in the presence of God and of Christ Jesus, who is to judge the living and the dead, and by His appearing and His kingdom: ²preach the word; be ready in season and out of season; reprove, rebuke, exhort, with great patience and instruction. ³For the time will come when they will not endure sound doctrine; but wanting to have their ears tickled, they will accumulate for themselves teachers in accordance to their own desires, ⁴and will turn away their ears from the truth and will turn aside to myths. ⁵But you, be sober in all things, endure hardship, do the work of an evangelist, fulfill your ministry (2 Timothy 4:1-5).

Let's focus on verse 5: *But you, be sober in all things, endure hardship, do the work of an evangelist, fulfill your ministry.* These four admonitions can be an excellent guide in our missionary purpose.

1) Be Sober

In this verse, the Greek word for "sober" is *nepho*. It means to be calm and collected in spirit. It is used in association with *watchfulness* and also refers to moral alertness.

This passage is a charge, a charge to "be calm and collected in our spirit." It is a charge to be spiritually watchful and alert to the moral strengths and decays around us. Be awake to the needs and opportunities that surround us. This takes place when we allow the Holy Spirit to have total control over our mind, body and spirit.

2) Endure Hardships

The Greek meaning for "endure hardships" in this passage is *kakopatheo,* which means "to suffer (endure) evils (hardships, troubles); to be afflicted."

Apparently we *will* go through hardships, and we must *endure* those hardships of life. Evils, troubles and afflictions are inevitable. Our posture must be one of endurance through spiritual strength. Being used by God in missions is not easy, but always rewarding.

3) Do the Work of Evangelism

"Work," or *ergon* in Greek, means "deed or act." This is a focus on the actual work of the ministry. We are charged to put boots on the ground, hands to the plow and invest talents into the work of missions.

The word "evangelism" used here is *euaggelistes,* meaning "bringer of good tidings, an evangelist; a messenger of good, a preacher of the Gospel; to proclaim good news." Evangelism spreads much wider than the pulpit. This evangelical work is greatly enhanced when those who are mission-minded actively do their portion with anointed passion.

4) Fulfill Your Ministry

"Fulfill" in Greek is *plerophoreo,* "to bear or bring full;

to make full; to carry through to the end, accomplish." This speaks to accomplishing the mission, completing the call, finishing the race and finding fulfillment through our obedient walk.

The word "ministry" used here is *diakonia* in Greek. It means "of those who, by the command of God, proclaim and promote religion among men; of domestic duties, of religious and spiritual ministration." This command directs us to proclaim and promote the Gospel to mankind, through spiritual administration and utilizing domestic duties in life.

Diversity in Missions

I will cover a few of the benefits of missions, but first, let's take an overview of what *short-term, mid-term* and *long-term* missions are and what each of them looks like.

Short-Term Missions

The duration of a short-term mission outreach will vary greatly, depending on the experience of the group leader and the current involvement of the church or organization that you are working with in missions. A short-term mission trip will commonly be between one and four weeks in duration, although some mission opportunities will span up to 90 days. These shorter mission outreaches are the most common and should not be seen as "lesser" in effectiveness or value.

When traveling to a foreign country, a 30-day to a 90-day work visa is commonly obtained. These longer commitments are most often comprised of professionals and/or students who can take up to a three-month break from school or work. Work visas must be applied for well in advance, but can open amazing doors of ministry for those who qualify. Through the medical field, educational field, construction, business consulting, etc., real mission work can take place by means of trades and skills. Never underestimate your ability, or the ability of others, to be used in missions by God.

When hosting a mission team, I often hear questions like, "What skills do we need to have on the team?"

I always answer, "We simply need people who are teachable, flexible and desire to be used of God." While there are those special projects that require the skills of a seasoned professional, don't exclude the others. There is plenty of kingdom work for every person, no matter his or her level of skill and experience. It's difficult to get an engineer excited about digging a ditch or raking a field, but I sure can get him pumped about drawing up some building specifications.

The most valuable tool anyone can bring to the mission field is a willing heart. In my experience, short-term missions will, by far, account for the largest army of missionaries. Because of the great flexibility and shorter investments of time and resources, these fit the mass of people whose specific calling will not land them in the next two categories.

Mid-Term Missions

Whereas a short-term mission can span up to 90 days in commitment, a mid-term mission will commonly start at 90 days and span up to a two-year commitment. This category has traditionally been the smallest of the three, but in recent years mid-term missions have become more popular due to the payoff for the missionary committing to these durations. In the three-month to two-year time, those in the field will see much more fruit from their labor.

Not only does this longer duration of time benefit the missionary who is going, it also greatly benefits the missionary in the field whom they are assisting. The long-term or, in some cases, full-term missionaries are truly grateful for any team for any amount of time if that team comes ready, flexible and focused.

The reality is, however, that missionaries find greater benefit from the longer commitments of others. The longer the time, the more they can count on the person or team. More can be invested and accomplished in that mission field. The host missionary will be prone to invest more teaching, training and opportunity into mid-term missionaries, simply due to their commitment of time.

While mid-term missions stand alone as a missions category, I would venture to say that a great percentage of those engaging in mid-term missions were first inspired while on a short-term mission trip. We see this process repeated over and over as we host mission teams to Alaska and see someone from that team receive the calling to come back for a mid-term missions trip. Often, in this way, the short-term and mid-term mission trips become stepping stones to long-term and full-term missionary work.

Long-Term Missions

Starting at a minimum of two years, long-term mission work often produces a lifetime commitment from the missionary. These are the only people who traditionally are allowed to hold the title of *missionary*. We have been trained up to believe that they are the "true" missionaries, and the rest of us simply aren't.

However, the missionary title is not what separates them. It's simply the duration of time. This group has an equal calling with the other two groups, but their call keeps them in the field longer, to fulfill a lasting work. Without the host missionary, who has researched the culture firsthand, the other two groups would struggle to find maximum success. A short-term or mid-term mission team can do wonderful ministry work in the field. But with the sustaining ability of the long-term missionary, that work can have great potential to grow and mature. Yes, we can receive a vision of a mission field from the comfort of our home. But to embrace, support and resource the matured vision that has been cultivated by a long-term missionary in the field, that partnership is priceless.

Missions Benefits

Although we learned, in 1 Corinthians 3:8, that the spiritual rewards are the same no matter what part we play in missions, we find that there are some immediate benefits that often take place for those who physically venture out on a missions outreach. Time for a healthy bowl of **R.I.C.E.**

Revelation:

Personal revelation is imperative to the follower of Jesus. Without it, we live off of information, becoming a conduit of religious thinking, at best. The Word of God is designed to become revelatory in our lives, transforming our very being. Although these times of personal revelation can take place anywhere, the mission field postures the heart and spirit to better hear these heavenly nuggets.

rev·e·la·tion

1. the act of revealing or disclosing; disclosure
2. something revealed or disclosed, especially a striking disclosure, as of something not before realized
3. Theology
   a. God's disclosure of Himself and His will to His creatures
   b. an instance of such communication or disclosure
   c. something thus communicated or disclosed

d. something that contains such disclosure, as the Bible

Impartation:

The impartations that take place in the field are unique to that mission field. You can show people your photos, play your videos and tell some exciting mission stories, but they will never really understand until their own boots hit the ground. The impartations that come from being on location simply can't be regenerated away from that mission field.

For the team member, these heavenly implants of mission passion, spiritual understanding and loving compassion become interwoven into his or her thinking and way of life. When the Holy Spirit has the missionary's attention, that information becomes personal, and at that point in time, the heart is open to receive and keep impartation.

Confirmation:

Sometimes people need to experience a taste of their purpose to recognize God's voice in that area of their life. Confusion will often be made clear when their boots hit the field and their eyes see what may have remained just a half-heard story, had they not gone.

Each year we specifically pray that the Holy Spirit will direct to us those whom God has already called to our state or region.

One of the first things I ask potential interns is,

"Where do you believe God is calling you?" If they have a calling to reach the Hispanic community, I recommend they apply to an internship that will focus on that calling, maybe something with a focus on that particular cultural group.

We open the door to everyone who is seeking an Alaska mission experience, and when we connect with those called to Alaska, we are helping them position themselves to hear that confirming word from the Lord.

Expansion:

When people experience a mission field that is blessed with God's favor, the borders of their heart will be expanded, and the fertile ground will nurture and expand their vision and faith. When they step into the arena of mission work, a greater understanding of the reality of missions will be birthed, inspiring them to pursue their heavenly calling.

When the goal of your short-term missions trip is to build, construct or do maintenance in the field, then a "work team" will be in order. The work team becomes a wonderful entry level for a first-time mission experience. As I covered in the first chapter, when I say "entry level," I don't mean "lesser" in ministry importance. These entry-level missions are excellent opportunities, especially for men who have bought into the lie that they are not missionaries and they can't do real ministry if they don't preach. It's common for us to hear these men tell their friends, family and co-workers that they are joining a "work team" to do some volunteer construction. However, they return from the field telling those same people about their "missionary trip."

Their view of what they were actually doing, and their overall view of what mission work really is, had been fundamentally changed. From the vantage point of the mission field, this expanded sight will open the heart to serve and do the work of the missionary at home and abroad. The pew will become less comfortable, and the fields, ready for harvest, will be calling their names.

CHAPTER THREE
PREPARATION OF PRAYER

*With all prayer and petition pray at all times in the Spirit,
and with this in view, be on the alert with all perseverance
and petition for all the saints. (Ephesians 6:18)*

Prayer Bear

It had been at least two days since our team had slept,
and we had spent some sleepless nights working on boat
motors and packing supplies for this daunting trek. The
next island that had functional camping potential would
be the first landing location for our small fleet of boats.
I'm sure I'll see one, just around the next bend, I would tell
myself. Even though it was our first leg of this mission,
sleep was a priority.

Mission Accomplished

The Yukon River will eat up an inattentive boat pilot. It is no place to navigate overloaded boats while fighting to keep your eyes open. Getting my team to a safe place for rest, food and prayer was my focus. The island that I was looking for was worth hunting down: It had high riverbanks, a graveled area big enough for several tents and a large fire. It also had good visibility to spot predators. Finally, I spotted it.

There wasn't much discussion after securing the boats to the rocky shore. Just working together, in silence, to make camp. My last order to the team was, "Nobody make a sound until I wake you." Not one complaint was made from the exhausted team: Those words were like music to their ears. The young missionary team fell fast asleep as soon as each member crawled into the tents. Not even the daylight (24/7 in the Alaskan summer) was a distraction to sleeping, and the only noises that could be heard were a slight breeze blowing through the trees and the river turning in the background. We entered our tents sometime after 4 a.m., and it remained totally silent throughout the day, until I sounded the wake-up bell around 1 p.m. Well, actually, it was a 12-gauge shotgun, the best camping alarm I could think of at the time (not a recommended alarm for home use).

The day was to be devoted to prayer and intercession, in preparation for ministry in the next village. The plan was to head downriver around mid-morning the next day. But today was about preparing our hearts, minds and focus.

PREPARATION OF PRAYER

Spending time in unified prayer before we minister has become non-negotiable. With the campfire burning (to keep the bugs at bay), our bellies full of MREs (meals ready to eat) and fresh camp coffee in hand, we were ready for some intense prayer time. I began by doing my usual motivational speech before prayer. Any leader knows the drill. I tried my best to paint a picture of our purpose, plan and strategy for the Alaska Native village we would visit the next day.

There we were, 14 camp chairs circling the fire like a wagon train, as I unsuccessfully kept trying to keep their attention. Two of my staff kept looking behind them, into the trees, and their nervousness had become obvious to everyone. Earlier, as we were just getting started, we had heard a large animal running through the water on the other side of the island. To regain the attention of the group, I quickly suggested that what we had heard was likely a young moose, nothing to be concerned about.

It's not exactly true that I was "losing" the focus of the team because I don't think I ever had it. Now, with two of my staff looking over their shoulders, a functional prayer time was a lost cause.

"Do you want me to go see what's over there?!" I blurted out in frustration to Charis and Jamie, two of my staff.

"YES," was the resounding answer.

We had lost a day catching up on much-needed sleep, and by now, I was intensely eager to get this team going, get us unified and get the show on the road (or on the river). I walked over to the trees, expecting to scare off an overly irritating porcupine. I wanted us to get focused and get back on schedule. The porcupine, however, was nowhere to be found. Instead I was aggressively greeted by a black bear. I was thinking, *Oh, great! Now we'll never get back to our prayer time.* You think it's distracting when those cell phones go off during prayer? Try a bear!

Black bears can often be turned around by using some deep, loud noises and waving of hands to appear intimidating. If that doesn't work, a good pelting of rocks can help. However, this bear must have been hungry — he continued to walk toward me with confidence. We were remote enough that this bear had not yet encountered humans, so he had no reason to be afraid.

The rocks pelting his body at close range, however, finally did the trick. He walked back into the thick brush of the forest.

I quickly headed back to the fire pit and began rounding up my team, who were by now very much awake. I was thinking, *I'll have their attention now.*

But before we could get settled back into our camp chair prayer circle, I heard one of the students yelling, "It's in the tent! The bear is in the tent!" Maria was pointing to our big, brand-new eight-man tent from Cabela's.

I quickly ran to the left side of the tent as others were pointing to the right. As I peeked around the corner, I could only see the rear end of the bear. He had made himself a custom door and was enjoying his hunt for food. He seemed to be completely focused on his mission and undistracted by our noise and commotion. Only a few yards away, I yelled as loud as I could, "Get out!" and the bear jumped out of the tent and bolted away from me like a scared rabbit. At about 40 yards away, he suddenly put on the brakes, just like in the cartoons.

After skidding to a halt, he turned around and stared me down, as if thinking, *Why am I running from this guy? I can take him.* Keeping his eyes fixed on me, he started walking back straight for me. By this time, my .44 Magnum was already out of its holster and pointed in his direction. He had his chance to run. This bear could have left and lived a full life. But here he was moving toward me with attitude.

So what did I, the missionary team leader, do? Well, keep in mind that this bear had just put a man-sized hole in our new Cabela's tent. He had destroyed a brand-new-out-of-the-box, first-time-in-use tent from Cabela's! When you are in bush Alaska, your tent is your home. It keeps the life-sucking Alaskan-sized mosquitoes from draining the last of your personal blood supply from you while you sleep. To destroy a man's tent in a remote location like this comes with a high penalty. Before he could get any closer to me, I squeezed the trigger and watched the 320-grain bear-load bullet make one fast and fatal entrance through the neck and chest of the black bear.

The impact of the projectile sent the bear and all of his aggression moving in the other direction. He did a complete flip, maneuvered a few yards off toward the river and quickly expired from the fatal wounds. Gotta love a clean kill. "Welcome to missions in Alaska!"

Now there was good news and bad news. The good news is that we would be enjoying fresh black bear meat for the next few days. The bad news is that our prayer schedule was shot, along with the bear.

My ministry experience has trained my mind to think in levels, and even before the trigger was pulled, I was contemplating the meat processing that would be in order. My initial hesitation to dispatch this bear was not based on concern for his feelings, but on the fact that the processing of this animal, legally and without wasted meat, would take priority over my schedule. Now, here I was, looking at the bear on the ground with no clue on how to properly dress it out. I had field dressed more than a dozen moose, several caribou and countless smaller game, but never a bear.

Then I remembered that the chief of the village where we were heading had a family fish camp just upriver, about 15 miles from us on the north bank of the Yukon. I decided to take a quick trip to the camp and ask him to teach me how to properly skin a bear.

His older brother was glad to help and quickly showed me how to do the job. In fact, he made it look easy. In return for his help, I gifted his family's camp with bear meat, which blessed them so much that the stories of the encounter and the gifting of fresh meat made its way to the village before we arrived there the next day. We served up the bear to our team and several elders that first day in the village. Who would have thought that killing that disruptive bear would be used to bless people, encourage a family and open up doors of ministry?!

Today, when I look at that bear hide hanging on my bedroom wall, I'm not reminded of a hunting experience. I'm reminded of just how many times the enemy will attempt to distract us from our purpose. He is frightened of our unified prayer because he knows the damage inflicted on the kingdom of hell when God's people pray.

The thief comes only to steal and kill and destroy; I came that they may have life, and have it abundantly (John 10:10).

Prayer Bear, as we now call him, represents what the enemy will do to the church, if tolerated. Because of his distracting presence, our focus will be taken away from our purpose, and our energy will be directed in defense mode instead of a mode of offense.

… who by faith conquered kingdoms, performed acts of righteousness, obtained promises, shut the mouths of lions, ³⁴quenched the power of fire, escaped the edge of the sword, from weakness were made strong, became mighty in war, put foreign armies to flight. ³⁵Women received back their dead by resurrection; and others were tortured, not accepting their release, so that they might obtain a better resurrection (Hebrews 11:33-35).

It's time we learn how to:

"Shut the mouth of the lion."
His strength is in his jaw. Shut tight the mechanism

intended to devour us. This is preventive spiritual maintenance, stopping the enemy before he gets started.

"Remove the power of the fire."

As we obey the voice of God, we are actually drenching the flames of destruction. Speaking the words of God will extinguish the fire and its power to destroy.

"Dodge the blade of the sword."

Spiritual strength and agility develop through our faith in action. Wisdom gives us flexibility and sensitivity to the Holy Spirit, to know when to duck, turn, run or fight.

"Become mighty warriors."

As He did with Gideon, God makes warriors out of undeserving men. He qualifies us and gives us a proactive vision to move obediently forward.

"Cast fear into our enemies."

Our fear of God will translate into the enemy fearing us.

"See the supernatural."

Expect all that the enemy has stolen from us will be given back. Expect the miraculous!

"Stand tall in our call, no matter the abuse."

Never give up, never back down, always obey … and always pray!

The Bear's Agenda

The bear will use <u>your weakness</u> to attempt to do three things in your life, to your calling, to your purpose and to your next missions endeavor. He comes to bring <u>fear</u>, <u>intimidation</u> and <u>hibernation</u>. Let's take a look at these three areas of attack.

Fear

Like erosion under the roads of life, fear will undermine your faith.

The bear brings fear because he knows that when a victim is overcome by fear, it will stop him dead in his tracks. Fear keeps you from rational thinking, it keeps you from hearing the voice of God and moving in authority. Fear can literally freeze you in place, both physically and spiritually. I recall a nightmare I would have as a child. I was so afraid of the monstrous enemy coming at me, yet I could not run, as if my feet were stuck to the ground.

Fear will kill your faith.

Fear can keep you right where you are at, fearful of forward movement. Fear of budget, fear of people, fear of dangers, fear of the future, fear of change. The enemy knows that if he can cause you to live in fear, you will struggle to walk in obedience to the call, voice and direction of Father God.

2 Timothy 1:7: For God has not given us a spirit of fear, but of power and love and of a sound mind (NKJV).

Intimidation

Webster's meaning of *intimidate*: "to make timid or fearful."

The bear will cause you to be intimidated because intimidation will keep you from being courageous, taking risks and stepping out in faith. Intimidation will most often manifest as a fear of a personality or position in your life. When you are intimidated, your ability to speak the truth of the Gospel is muted by the enemy. The goal of intimidation is to keep your mouth closed!

Intimidation comes from thinking less of God and less of His power in you. The enemy can keep your mouth closed from speaking the truth as long as you think he is stronger than you. When you understand the strength and power of God in you, the bear has no intimidating power over you. When you recognize who you really are in Christ, then, like young David, you become the intimidator rather than the intimidated.

Hibernation

The bear will influence you to hibernate. Hibernation is a survival instinct for the bear. But it becomes a place of hiding for the follower of Christ. Hibernation puts your dreams to sleep and keeps you from stepping into your intended kingdom destiny. It takes the vision given to you by God and barricades it for a season of time. Many believers have a "vision" that is buried deep underground, hibernating, decaying and often dying.

The bear den is a dark place with no light to penetrate

its cover. It is claustrophobic and constricting to any movement. The only way to see the light is by busting out of this prison barricade and stepping into the light.

Therefore I am well content with weaknesses, with insults, with distresses, with persecutions, with difficulties, for Christ's sake; for when I am **weak**, *then I am* **strong** *(2 Corinthians 12:10).*

Please fully understand this reality: The enemy hates your mission. He will bring fear into your planning if your faith is weak. He will use intimidation effectively if your trust in the Lord is weak. If you operate in your own strength, he will have the opportunity to influence you to bury your vision into deep hibernation.

Four powerful steps of bear defense:

1) Activate Your Faith

For just as the body without the spirit is dead, so also faith without works is dead (James 2:26).

Build your faith by putting it into action. In other words, put your feet into what you believe. Faithlessness will posture you for fear, and fear will keep you from conquering the predators attacking your purpose. Fear will always undermine your faith.

But fear in one's life is actually not the foundational issue: It's a lack of love that gives room for fear to take its deceptive grip. As we learn to love as Christ loves us, fear leaves at the same pace. Perfect love casts out fear.

By this, love is perfected with us, so that we may have

confidence in the day of judgment; because as He is, so also are we in this world. *¹⁸There is no fear in love; but perfect love casts out fear, because fear involves punishment, and the one who fears is not perfected in love. ¹⁹We love, because He first loved us (1 John 4:17-19).*

And remember: Your faith without your works is dead.

Faithlessness will posture you for fear, and fear will keep you from conquering the predators attacking your destiny.

2) Trust God

I will say to the Lord, "My refuge and my fortress, my God, in whom I trust!" (Psalm 91:2).

Make sure that Jesus is the cornerstone and rock of your fortress. If your trust is built on any other thing, person or system, you will fail in life and ministry. Rebel against the temptation to lean on your experience, your talents, your resources or your intellect. Without a complete trust in the Lord, these things will only get in the way of your purpose and potentially be used against you by the enemy.

⁵Trust in the Lord with all your heart, and do not lean on your own understanding. ⁶In all your ways acknowledge Him, and He will make your paths straight. ⁷Do not be wise in your own eyes; fear the Lord and turn away from evil. ⁸It will be healing to your body, and refreshment to your bones (Proverbs 3:5-8).

Put ALL your trust in the Lord! Trusting any other

source will leave you empty and feeling insecure. Insecurity conditions the heart for intimidation. Simply put, the insecure are easily intimidated.

The boy David could not have run toward his giant of an enemy if he was dealing with insecurity. He showed confidence in the power of God, and he was secure that his Father God was with him all the way.

3) Empower Your Vision

Empower your vision with obedience. Your vision needs legs; it needs YOU to respond to it with forward movement. It can't move forward on its own.

Many have a "heavenly vision" that they hold in their heart and never see it come to pass, while they make excuses and even reason with God over it. Some are even tempted to alter His plan or give God conditions.

I know a husband and wife who have declared their calling to the mission field for decades. But business ventures, financial preparing and other investment obligations have kept them safe and secure at home, only talking about their missions call rather than living it. Sure, they might answer that call one day. But how many years were lost because they never empowered that vision?

Disobedience to the vision of God actually puts the vision in hibernation. The act of obedience will bust your heavenly purpose out of its grave and into the light of truth.

4) Kill the Bear

Simply make a decision to kill the bear! You won't find it recorded where David "reasoned" with the lion, and he didn't simply ignore the bear and hope it would leave his sheep alone. Nor did he choose to sit the giant down on a sofa and "counsel" him.

He knew that if he tolerated any of the three, the problem would not go away but rather escalate into mass panic, confusion and, ultimately, death. David knew the lion would not be content with a feast of just one lamb. He knew the bear would spread fear and scatter the flock. And he knew the giant would cause God's people to run in fear and forget the greatness of their God and His prophetic call on their lives and nation.

Toleration and procrastination are the brothers of failure.

Your servant has killed both the lion and the bear; and this uncircumcised Philistine will be like one of them, since he has taunted the armies of the living God (1 Samuel 17:36).

The Final Blow

I was on the dock, supervising the unloading of some much-needed gear that was just boated into this remote camp. It was a warm summer evening on the upper Yukon River, and my mind was focused on the flight that I needed to take early the next morning. It had taken weeks to secure this private charter.

PREPARATION OF PRAYER

"Hey, Pastor Ron! There's that bear!" yelled one of my staff. Sure enough, there he was, swimming across the river from an island, and I was sure he would be heading to the back side of our camp.

This particular animal had been in and out of our camp for weeks, and he was becoming aggressively more confident with each visit. He was a large adult, with a rare DNA that set him apart from his other companions.

He was what they call a "cinnamon black bear." These black bears are found in less than 5 percent of the 100,000 black bears in the state. According to the Native elders, the cinnamon or "chocolate bears," as some locals call them, are much more aggressive than their all black relatives. Apparently these predators were born with an extra strand of angry in their DNA.

I had a hunch where this critter would be heading next. I guessed that he would use the ancient trail on the tree line north of camp and work his way back to us in the cover of the trees. "Can I come with you?" one of our summer interns asked.

"Not this time," I replied. "I need to do this alone." It's not that I had Rambo syndrome. I just knew that one person could get into that trail with much more stealth than two, and I would need to get to the right spot before my cover was blown.

I made it to the location I had intended to secure as quickly and quietly as possible and soon found myself standing in a junction of that old trail. While I was looking around for cover, I caught something move from the corner of my eye. That was him for sure, more than 100 yards off in the distance. I dropped to my right knee and rested my left elbow on my left knee. With my trusty Smith & Wesson .44 Magnum pointing in his general direction, I waited and waited, and then waited some more. Although I was in the middle of the trail with no immediate cover, I felt that I had the advantage. As he slowly moved toward me, I remained perfectly still with a tree line behind me.

Only my movement, noise or smell would give my position away. Upon arriving at the trail, I had done a quick wind test, grabbing some dust and tossing it in the air. My test had revealed zero wind in that area, which is good. Eighty yards … 75 yards … 65 yards and closing. At this point, I was suffering the consequences of not taking the time to grab my bug hat. The netting would have kept the hundreds of blood-sucking mosquitoes off my face and neck. I had to stay perfectly still and ignore the increasing pain — a pain, however, that would seem insignificant if compared to what this beast could do to me.

The bear had been moving slowly and steadily toward me, and then he suddenly stopped, as if alerted to something wrong. I knew he had not seen me, but his supernatural bear nose was somehow finding my scent in the airways. He didn't move any closer, but continued to turn his head from left to right and then back again. This is a common way they pinpoint their prey. By getting a read from left and right, they can accurately locate their next meal with their amazing sense of smell. A black bear can smell that next meal more than five miles away.

Sure, just leaving him alone would have been much easier. Procrastination is always much easier. The problem is that if we had continued to tolerate this predator, he would have gained boldness and strength over us. It could have been him on that trail waiting, quietly, to ambush one of us.

Apparently this big bear wanted a better view in my direction, and in attempting to do that, he made a fatal mistake. He stood up on his hind legs, pointing his nose up in the air to the left and to the right. Doubtful that I'd get a better opportunity than this, I slowly squeezed the trigger and released a bear slug into the air. I went temporarily deaf from the blast as the massive predator flipped over backward and hit the ground hard and loud. My range finder had put him at 37 yards, close enough for this missionary. The slug had drilled through the center of his mass, taking out his nervous system, and a second shot up close would make his dispatch quick and painless.

I was successful in harvesting the bear and removing the threat, but immediately began suffering the results of not being completely prepared. Sure, I knew what to do and had the experience with my pistol to complete it. But had I taken just a moment longer to put on my bug hat and insert my earplugs, what a difference it would have made. My neck, face and head were swollen from the hungry bugs, and a constant loud ringing was playing in my ears for what would be the next few days. Also, I wish I would have been wearing the GoPro camera. Wow, what a YouTube video that would be!

After the celebration of photo shoots and fresh bear backstrap, there was a new sense of peace over the camp. This bear had lost his power to bring fear, to intimidate or to influence any part of our purpose.

Our church culture has programmed us to let the giants "taunt" the armies of the living God. I propose to you that young David was more bothered by the non-responsiveness of the army than by the threat of the enemy. He could clearly see the taunting and knew that if tolerated, this enemy would secure victory over God's people. Sometimes you just need to kill the bear.

What bears are keeping you from your next outreach?

What is that bear doing effectively to keep you from your intended mission field?

What level of tolerance are you comfortable with?

Yes, the mission field is full of danger. Jesus never said, "Come follow me, and it will be easier for you." It's hard! That's why we call it "the *work* of the ministry." The greatest work of ministry we can do is also the one area we most often slack in. Maybe it's just me, but I must say, it's easy for me to get deep into the logistical and mechanical part of missions outreach and bypass the much-needed prayer. Often it's the many distractions we tolerate that feed our procrastination of prayer. But nothing of real value can be achieved without prayer.

Your obedience to the vision of God is worship unto the Lord. The voice of the Father is frequently found with greater clarity through prayer. Prayer conditions the heart to better recognize the voice of the Lord. Yes, there are times of crying out to the Lord. But more time should be spent on listening to Him. Some say, "God is such a great listener." Yes, He sure is. But His communication to us through the Holy Spirit is best received with our mouths closed and our ears open.

As we engage in these times of prayer, we are learning to hear and distinctly recognize the voice of the Lord. As we mature in this, we equally develop our discernment. A wonderful byproduct of knowing His voice is knowing when it *isn't* His voice. Divine or demonic? Discern the difference between heavenly appointments and enemy assignments.

Deceptive Web

Canadian Yukon Territory: We had been ministering there for several days as our team of 40 was on a three-week ministry outreach tour. The Convoy Of Worship (C.O.W.) tour was an annual outreach that we had conducted for eight years in a row. The C.O.W. tour was comprised of young people and adult leaders who were trained to serve churches and communities in a variety of ways. Ministry needs and local vision drove our purpose and daily schedule.

One of the local churches in Canada had asked us to

provide a few days of evangelistic youth outreach from a downtown location. This facility was privately owned, and the owner had shown a strong interest in hosting the youth ministry of this local church. The owner had created a "youth hangout" with video games, food, coffee, etc. Sounds like a great place to stage a youth outreach, right?

I planned to take my staff and check out the location the day before the event started. But first we needed to seek the Lord. Having never been in that city, culture or environment before, it was crucial to bathe this event in prayer. We spent several hours interceding for the community and asking for clear direction over the youth ministry outreach we were about to engage in.

After our preparation of prayer, we headed downtown to assess the building and grounds, meet the staff, confirm what we had access to utilize and form a plan for a successful outreach.

However, as we entered the threshold of that building, an overwhelming darkness came over us like a blanket. In the main room, we sensed what felt like a strong satanic presence, and as we investigated the decor, we saw many spider drawings on the walls.

There also was a large painting of what appeared to be a demonic being. When I inquired about the painting, the manager of the building told me it was his personal spirit guide, which he called by name. He explained that this spirit stayed with him day and night, influencing the direction of his path.

After a very short conversation, the manager quickly

went upstairs to his office loft. Hanging from the ceiling, directly under his loft, was a lifelike model of a black widow spider. This creature spanned the entire ceiling space of that corner of the room. It stretched more than 7 feet in length across the surface with many smaller spiders, some models and some painted, traveling down the wall and across the ceiling, moving away from it.

From this room we walked into the kitchen, looking for the owner who had invited the local youth pastor to use this location.

She seemed overly nervous to meet us and was reluctant to shake my hand. And immediately after I shook her hand, it was as if the Holy Spirit downloaded a series of video images through my mind. These videos were very detailed in content, and each one revealed what I believe were the owner's true motives. After this encounter, I gathered my team and headed back to the church.

Because of the prayer time, we were extra-sensitive to the voice of the Lord, and an increased state of discernment was operating through us. The average teen walking into this place might feel comfortable and maybe even at home. Not because of any loving atmosphere, but because of an insensitivity to its darkness.

I asked for a meeting with the pastoral staff and began to share what the Lord had shown me. You see, the purpose of this exposing was much bigger than our youth outreach. We would leave in a few days. But the owner and manager would be there for the long haul, and this new partnership was just a beginning. The warning was so detailed that the pastors had trouble believing me. They had some past history with the owner and knew she had rebellion issues, but to believe that she was into the demonic this deep was hard to swallow.

This youth hangout had become a very effective web of deception, I told him. Food, games and freedom from other adults was the magnet. Then the spider could do its work. This spider was in the form of a woman, the owner, who I told him had been seducing teen boys into sexual activity. The manager was deep into the occult, and he made sure the spiritual environment was accommodating to entice teens in that arena.

The pastors accepted my strong advice to sever any partnership with this woman and discourage their youth from visiting this place, even though they thought I was exaggerating the story or being overly sensitive. Several months later, the lead pastor called me and said, "You were completely right! She was exposed, and all of those things were happening!"

After the call ended, I was reminded of just how important prayer is for successful ministry. Not just a prayerful heart on your missions trip, but I'm talking about being pre-prayed up before your missionary boots hit the field. Being prepared is being pre-prayed.

The enemy will take advantage of unpreparedness at any level, and the area most often in need of more preparation is prayer. Though I personally pray, and I understand that my continual communication with the

Lord is necessary to both understand His leading and accomplish the task, I must say that prayer does not come natural to me. Scheduling times of team prayer and collective intercession and fasting for an event usually come from my greatest prayer warrior, my wife, Yolanda. She often says, "Intercession is entering into a session of prayer on behalf of another."

On the topic of the importance of prayer, I want you to hear from her:

> Prayer is preparation. Prayer makes things happen. Prayer opens the doors to heaven.
>
> Prayer is communication with our Heavenly Father. Prayer prepares the way before us.
>
> I always think of prayer as communing with the Lord. You're communicating, loving on God, sharing your heart and learning His heart.
>
> Prayer is a command in the Word to all the saints. When you read the life of Jesus, how many times do we read that He went off to pray? He went off to be with His Father. The night before His crucifixion, He went off to the garden to pray. What did He pray? Jesus was praying for Himself that He could withstand the laying down of His life, go through with obeying His Heavenly Father until death: "Not My will but Your will be done." Now, if Jesus, the Son of God who has the power of God in Him, the power to speak and it's done, had to pray for Himself to stay within His Father's will, how much more do we need to pray for ourselves to do God's will?
>
> Before every outreach we spend focused time

in prayer, many times fasting and praying together as a team. We pray for ourselves, for God to bring in provision, for increased anointing of the Holy Spirit, for walls to be broken down in the souls to which we minister, to hear the voice of God, for souls saved, for protection and for all of God's will to happen.

Prayer is needed at the very beginning and through to the end of every event, asking God to open up doors of opportunity and show us where we are supposed to go. We hear from God and then plan our outreach. You really can't effectively move forward without prayer.

Again, prayer is communication with the Lord. It opens up the doors to hear His voice and gives us a passion to go where He wants us to go. Throughout the Bible we read of men and women spending time with God, then hearing His voice. We read how God gives instruction to the men and women of God, but then they have to pray to make God's will happen.

In the Bible, we have many examples of how men and women were called to pray and the miracles that occurred as a result of that prayer. God told Elijah to pray for rain. Elijah prayed and prayed, he even had someone check to see if rain was coming. And he continued to pray until the answer came. Daniel. I love Daniel, a man who had favor from God and a man who bowed down and prayed three times a day. He fasted and prayed, and God showed him things to come. He could interpret dreams through inquiring of the Lord.

PREPARATION OF PRAYER

Our greatest example is Jesus. We read many times how Jesus went away to pray to His Heavenly Father. It was after fasting and praying in the desert that Jesus came out and started preaching and doing miracles. This shows the "power increase" when we spend time alone with God.

Intercession

When we go to prayer on behalf of someone else, that is intercession.

Intercession (Webster's dictionary):
1. an act or instance of interceding
2. an interposing or pleading on behalf of another person
3. a prayer to God on behalf of another
4. to act or interpose on behalf of someone in difficulty or trouble, as by pleading or petition: *to intercede with the governor for a condemned man*

I looked for someone among them who would build up the wall and stand before Me in the gap on behalf of the land so I would not have to destroy it, but I found no one (Ezekiel 22:30).

To me this verse describes intercession. God looked for one person to stand before Him and in place of that wicked city to ask Him not to destroy it, ask Him to save it. But He found no one. If He would have found one person, He would not have destroyed it. But He found no one. So He had to destroy it.

MISSION ACCOMPLISHED

This shows the power of intercession. This shows the power of standing in the gap and asking for salvation for a person, building walls of protection, deliverance and salvation around him or her. God will hear the cries of His people. He just wants that one person to stand in the gap.

Gap (Webster's dictionary):
1. a space between two people or things
2. a hole or space where something is missing
3. a missing part

As a visual learner, I picture intercession as a person in battle. God is on one side, the devil is on the other and the person is in the middle but not able to fight on his own. So, as we intercede, we step in the middle between God and the devil and pray on behalf of that person. We pray what he should be praying but is not wanting to or is not strong enough to at that time. We are praying for strength, victory, deliverance and that he hears God's voice. I think of how "Jesus wept" — that was intercession on behalf of Lazarus.

One thing that we have come to learn is that when we go into an area or are standing in the gap in prayer, we can take on the emotions and feelings of the people group we are praying for. For example, when we enter a community where many people are dealing with suicide or rejection, self-hatred or hatred toward men, we have seen team members deal with these same emotional battles. When you are praying for someone, you can take on the very thing he or she is dealing with. So, pay attention when you experience warfare on a trip or you are praying specifically for a person. Many times you can sense their issues because you are being "made known" of their warfare so you will know how to pray for them. We can't keep the burdens that we are feeling for others on us. So turn these inward battles around in prayer, and pray for the people of that area. We need to rise up in the power and authority that Jesus Christ has given us and stand in the gap in prayer to save lives! Always seek the Holy Spirit for direction. Make yourself available to God to be a vessel the Holy Spirit can pray through. You can be that *one person* building up walls and standing in the gap on behalf of people.

When you pray, know that God hears you. Your prayers are going up to heaven and making a difference. Pray the Word of God. His Word does not return void!

We are on a mission, and we must go in prepared, filled with His Word and presence, being strengthened in the Lord and sensitive to His voice. This takes place when we are prayed up.

— Yolanda Pratt

Without the investment of prayer, we can find ourselves encountering situations that we just aren't ready for. As we call on the power of the Lord to go before us and make a way, the Holy Spirit does exactly that. When that road is not paved with the power of prayer, our mission work will be much more challenging. I recall times when it was necessary to pull the team away from the field and regroup for needed prayer. The need for these group prayer meetings will always be there. But how many of those times of retreat would not have been needed if we had first laid down a foundation of prayer?

Protecting Your Investments

When you protect your prayer times prior to your missions event, you are protecting the most valuable investment that you can make into your ministry. When we pre-pray, we are investing into the success of that mission! There are several priceless benefits that come with this investment of prayer:

1. Accurately hearing the voice and direction of the Lord, thus saving valuable time, resources and energy.
2. A unified front is cultivated, and a spirit of unity grows with every collective prayer encounter.
3. Anointed teamwork in the field. Through prayer, emotional and spiritual issues are dealt with at the home base, and a blanket of anointing will rest on the missions team.

With all prayer and petition pray at all times in the Spirit, and with this in view, be on the alert with all perseverance and petition for all the saints (Ephesians 6:18).

[16]Rejoice always; [17]pray without ceasing; [18]in everything give thanks; for this is God's will for you in Christ Jesus (1 Thessalonians 5:16-18).

Demon Run

It was just one of those days ... starting with a rough night's sleep on a cold concrete church floor. After getting ready for the morning in an undersized church restroom, I woke up my team and headed to the kitchen. I knew that the volunteers who were kindly making our team breakfast would have made some coffee. "Please, Lord, let there be coffee!" I quietly prayed. I could smell it as I turned the last corner to the kitchen area. Please forgive me, but in those days, I preferred my coffee strong, no cream and enough sugar to kill a hummingbird. I got my coffee and realized that the sugar dispenser was empty! One of the youth was kind enough to take it into the kitchen pantry and fill it up. Yes! Now I can get kick-started! I'm not sure why, but instead of sipping it, my plan was to chug the first cup and quickly follow it with a second. After all, we had some set-up and much ministry prep to do.

Sugar is sweet, but salt is NOT! This young man had mistaken salt for sugar, and after the first gulp, I was spewing hot salted coffee on the floor! Just for your information, I'm not a chemist, but there must be some sort of chemical reaction that takes place when salt encounters coffee. Trust me, don't try this at home. When that combination enters your mouth, something very, very wrong happens. Anything I put into my mouth tasted overly salty for a week.

It was our San Francisco Outreach: one week of intense street ministry with two dozen youth and leaders. Part of this outreach involved providing an outdoor event in the Haight-Ashbury part of the city. This famous intersection has some interesting history and even more interesting people who choose to live on the streets in that area. I had prearranged some professional foot-baggers, known as "hacky sackers" to us nonprofessionals, to perform a free exhibition that would draw a crowd, which it did very well. Reaching these people with the love of Jesus was the goal, and that's what we busied ourselves doing.

Not an hour into the event, I could sense someone staring me down. You know that creepy feeling you are being watched? Well, here I was, standing to the side of the stage during the performance with more than 100 people around us, and yet something felt off, like eyes were burning a hole in my head.

As I glanced over the audience, my eyes went across the street and up the hill to a small group of street people who were gathered there. Even though this group was more than a football field away, my eyes locked with those of a very large man. His eyes literally seemed to be beaming, and just then, when he realized I had spotted him, he bolted straight for me.

It didn't take him long to shorten the gap and begin bursting through the tight crowd of spectators. When he got within 10 feet of me, the hands of this man stretched out to grab me, like some demonic monster in a horror movie.

As my mind quickly processed my options, I went with the most practical one: I ran! This giant, Lurch-like man chased me around and around the stage until I finally lost him in the crowd. Near the end of the event, I could see him running through the park as if he had a lead on me.

I had escaped death! Okay, maybe dismemberment. At the very least, I had escaped embarrassment. No, I don't think Jesus would have run, but I sure didn't have time to pull out my "What Would Jesus Do?" card and inquire of the Lord. That time of inquiring would have served me best prior to this mission.

I believe a greater investment of fasting and prayer could have, and would have, paved the way for a much different ending to this story.

[14] When they came to the crowd, a man came up to Jesus, falling on his knees before Him and saying, [15] "Lord, have mercy on my son, for he is a lunatic and is very ill; for he often falls into the fire and often into the water. [16] I brought him to Your disciples, and they could not cure him." [17] And Jesus answered and said, "You unbelieving

and perverted generation, how long shall I be with you? How long shall I put up with you? Bring him here to Me." [18] And Jesus rebuked him, and the demon came out of him, and the boy was cured at once.

[19] Then the disciples came to Jesus privately and said, "Why could we not drive it out?" [20] And He said to them, "Because of the littleness of your faith; for truly I say to you, if you have faith the size of a mustard seed, you will say to this mountain, 'Move from here to there,' and it will move; and nothing will be impossible to you. [21] But this kind does not go out except by prayer and fasting" (Matthew 17:14-21).

The Recipe of Missions

When you are preparing a recipe, there are ingredients that can be substituted, and there are ingredients that should never be replaced.

In the recipe for "Successful Missions," prayer is one of those non-negotiable ingredients. Intercessional prayer is a foundational ingredient. Without it, the recipe will fail. "Unified Prayer" is a powerful part of your planning and preparation. Schedule it throughout your planning, building a strong intercessional foundation that will lead to your executing your mission with success.

Chapter Four
Raising Funds

²⁷Whoever does not carry his own cross and come after Me cannot be My disciple. ²⁸For which one of you, when he wants to build a tower, does not first sit down and calculate the cost to see if he has enough to complete it? ²⁹Otherwise, when he has laid a foundation and is not able to finish, all who observe it begin to ridicule him.
(Luke 14:27-29)

Counting the Costs

Two airplanes were scheduled to land in a nearby village, transporting much-needed food and supplies. I confirmed the flight departures on the satellite phone and was excited about personally picking up this special cargo. I had not seen my amazing wife for several weeks, and she would be accompanying these shipments.

Having run this stretch of the river countless times, I knew that boating the 30 river miles should take less than an hour. Wanting to be there, waiting at the airstrip for Yolanda, I left our youth camp early. The boat had been stripped down of any excess weight by my request as I knew I would be hauling a maximum load on my trek back upriver.

The weather was great: low wind, great water and warm afternoon sun beaming down on me. Thirty minutes into my journey, I began to notice a lack of power output. Jumping into the standard operation for this, I killed the motor and checked the jet unit for blockage. It checked out in good working condition.

It must be a bad spark plug, I thought. As I fired up the engine, an overwhelming noise came from under the engine cover. *Oh, no!* After lifting the cover, it was apparent that the problem was bigger than a spark plug. I could actually feel a piston rod slamming violently against the inside of the cylinder.

Remember that I had asked my team to lighten up the boat? Well, they did a great job: Somebody had even removed both paddles. Also, I had been meaning to attach a longer rope to the front of the boat. The tie-off rope that I had was long enough to tie to a dock but not long enough to throw to a shore.

Let me paint a picture for you.

There I was, alone, with no paddles, no backup motor and free-floating down the turbulent Yukon River. Talk about being "up a creek." I could get stuck on some remote sandbar or sucked into a cut bank and capsize the craft.

Stuff happens in missions, and looking back, I must say we need these challenges for perspective. Without a reference point from the bottom, we will never appreciate the view from the top.

Only the bare bones of emergency equipment could be found in the boat: life preserver, raincoat, fire starter and my trusty handgun. Among these things was the one thing I was glad to have with me: a satellite phone.

In this part of the world, you could actually be lost for days or even weeks before someone finds you, if they find you at all. So I make it a habit to pack the satellite phone with me when going it alone. I had floated down for some time and now was only three miles from my village destination. The hard turn up the north channel would be a real challenge. Thankfully, as the boat spun downriver, it stayed near the north bank and kept just far enough away to avoid slamming into it.

I made calls to the village and finally reached someone who was glad to get into his boat and assist me. If I passed the village, I would have to keep this craft afloat until the next village, 90 miles downriver. I knew the motor was shot and decided to fire it up one last time to get me headed into the mouth of this smaller channel leading to the village.

My wife was happy to see me eventually arrive at the village, and needless to say, I was so very glad to see her. We arranged for another boat to come downriver and transport all the supplies. After one intense day of field logistics and $14,000 expended, the mission continued on.

Things will happen in the field. There's no way around it. And ministry is not cheap! Some mission endeavors may cost more than others, but every mission will cost you. The more remote you take your missions work, the higher the cost will climb.

Every year we get a team or two that calls us in hopes of finding an "economy mission trip," a trip that will allow them to "afford" to do missions in Alaska. Do you think you can't afford to invest into missions? Really? Actually, you can't afford not to.

This mandate we have, the mandate to take part in missions, is very costly mentally, physically, spiritually and, yes, financially. When we use our "available funds" as a final guide to our mission field commitment, we propagate a dangerous lesson of faithlessness that keeps people comfortable warming the pews of our churches.

Provision or Problem?

They were slowly navigating toward the shoreline as we pulled up to the bank of the river, with our trucks pulling the boats. Two German men were on holiday and had started their adventure in Whitehorse, Canada, where they bought supplies and built a large raft. This mini-barge was their home for the weeks of traveling down the Yukon River. I took a walk over to greet these river travelers, while my team began our usual procedure of unloading the trucks and getting the boats ready to launch.

A two-month mission in Germany with my wife in 1988 left me with just enough exposure to recognize that these two men were from Deutschland. Although their English was much better than my German, conversation was a bit challenging.

After a few minutes, it became clear that they wanted to sell me their raft. Wow! I had never bought a giant homemade raft before, but the timing couldn't have been better. They were ending their trek, and we were just getting started with ours.

This boat launching was crucial, as we were building and running the first year of a summer youth camp in the area known as the Gwich'in Athabascan region called "Camp Nahshii." (More on this camp later.) We had depleted all of our resources just to get this far, and we were in need of everything: tools, gear, camp supplies and, yes, food. We had come this far chasing a vision God had given us, and we were sure that God would supply our needs.

The Germans were well prepared for their journey and had actually overstocked supplies.

After some negotiations, they were happy to take $75 and a ride to town (170 miles) in exchange for the rig and all its supplies. This was perfect for us and them since our drivers were heading back to Fairbanks, anyway.

"Auf Wiedersehen!"

After getting them on their way, we inspected the loot.

Wow! Tools, gear, camping supplies, clothing and pounds upon pounds of food! This 12-by-24-foot raft had a full cabin on top, supported by 28 55-gallon drums for flotation. We would be needing a floating boat dock at the camp, so this monster would be a real blessing if we could just get it 150 miles downriver.

Have you ever had a blessing turn into a curse? Well, maybe curse is a bit harsh. But this wonderful blessing had another side.

It's not because a problem was built into the deal, but mostly because the leader of this group was in a little over his head and not quite experienced enough for this next leg of the adventure.

We had never pulled a raft downriver but I thought, *How hard could it be?* This year, 2009, would be the first year for our remote camp: We had a mandate to get there!

Balancing the boat loads was easier now that we had access to this large raft. We formulated a plan and launched our collage of watercraft down the river. After traveling a short distance from the village, however, it became alarmingly apparent that we were not steering the raft. The raft was steering us!

Jet boats serve a great purpose in the many shallows of this river, but using them as tugboats is dysfunctional at best. No matter how hard we pulled in one direction, that beast of a houseboat would pull us the other way. After digging our convoy out of a few shallow areas, we were ultimately forced into what later would be found to be a massive, shallow side channel. This slow and long taper in the river simply did not have the depth needed to get us through. With crashing force, both boats wrapped around the now-shipwrecked raft. We had only traveled 20 of the 150 miles to camp, and we were in a mess.

After spending some time looking over our situation, a plan of escape emerged. "When I pull your boat out, I will be at full power. It's imperative that you quickly pull in the rope after we cut it!" I repeated this order a few times, and then it was time to open the throttle. The boat broke free as planned, but the recovery of rope was not as fast as the suction of the jet unit. When a jet shaft has 30 feet of marine rope wrapped around it, you have idle power at best.

Slowly we made our way the 70 miles downriver to the next village, leaving Jonathan behind, along with a student, to watch over the raft. The next village, Fort Yukon, would be Jonathon's new home because he was moving there to be its new youth pastor. Being stranded in the middle of nowhere on a raft was a great introduction to his new village life. After several boat trips to transfer the supplies from the raft to the village, the raft was salvaged of any usable parts, then left alone on the river. Years later this massive craft of provision and problem would be spotted farther downriver resting high and dry on an island.

God blesses mission work. Why wouldn't He — it's His plan! Unfortunately, we don't always handle what He has given us with complete wisdom. We sometimes make a mess of what was intended to bless us.

Just like ours, your next mission outreach will cost you. We have established that mission work is not cheap. With the cost of travel increasing, the overall cost of traveling to missions can skyrocket. Here in Alaska, we regularly find that flights to the lower 48 and Hawaii are far less expensive than flying to a village within our own state. And even with the best planning, stuff will happen.

Another Boat Down

The supplies were loaded, and last-minute details were underway. We would be heading northeast any day now to launch these overloaded boats onto the Yukon River. Hours turned to days and days to weeks as we waited for the ice to break up on the river. Like many spring times before, we wait for the first report of ice breakup, head to where the road meets the river and then follow it downriver to our camp. Our problem was that this year the breakup was weeks late, and when it did break free, massive flooding in the entire region became our deterrent.

Visual reports of the boat launch in Circle (a small village from which we start our river travels) came back saying that the river was completely blocked off with building-sized walls of ice. The floodwaters had pushed ice over the bank and into the village. The only open boat launch was in the other direction, 300 miles downriver.

After a day of travel, we launched our loaded watercraft. It was only 150 miles upriver to the camp, about six to seven hours of boating, if all went well. With our third boat sitting in the yard with a blown motor, this trip would be made with only two.

We battled hard and long just to get 30 miles upriver to the first village, where we would leave one boat for needed parts and repairs. Clarence, one of my staff, was accompanied by Travis, a summer intern. The two would get parts and head up to meet us. That was the plan. Jared, another summer intern, and I would then try to make it alone, fighting the ice, trees and other massive debris coming toward us. We had a small team that was stranded at our camp, and with the water rising, they needed food and supplies soon.

Only 60 miles to go, but our forward movement had slowed considerably. With the river littered with debris, our jet unit had been severely damaged. A call on the satellite phone informed us of a mighty mass of ice coming our way: One of the major rivers had broken loose farther upriver. We found the back side of an island to wait it out, hoping the danger would pass by us. In our haste, we had left our supply of food and water on the other boat, so we were in survival mode.

But the rusty old 12 gauge and some much older shells in the boat would help us find food for the next few days — fresh mallard over a campfire is survival at its best. A large block of ice on the shore of our camp spot would be our fresh water source for a few days.

But then our little island camp began to shrink rapidly. I awoke to see the river only three feet from Jared's sleeping bag! It was time to abort the trip and regroup 90 miles downriver. With only idle power, we slowly coasted down to meet our drivers at the bridge.

After a mechanical inspection of the boat, we found that we would need to replace it with a new boat. I wasn't sure how this would happen, since we were already four weeks behind on camp preparations and way over maintenance budget.

Have you ever had every single plan you made fall apart? Well, this was one of those adventures. We finally made it to the camp with a new boat that the Lord miraculously provided. My comfortable cushion of getting to the camp a month early was not an option, but we did get there two days before the first camp started, and more importantly, God showed up!

Father God is the pro at vision, and He will supply the provision.

Even when all seems to go wrong, you press toward the mark. Through steps of faith and simply moving forward on a mission call, I have seen God provide in a plethora of ways, from checks in the mail, to items donated, to supplies and equipment delivered, to $100 bills shoved under the door of vehicles left in the yard with a key and note. God brings in the provision both supernaturally and practically, which brings us to the subject of fundraising.

Fundraisers

Like many preparing for a large ministry endeavor, I have reluctantly involved myself in "fundraiser" events, and more often than I care to admit, I have loathed the very idea.

Stay with me here. Yes, God can use the fundraiser. After all, He is God, and He can use anything He wants. But there was a question I asked myself during and after every fundraising event, no matter how successful: "Why am I doing this?"

I believe this question stayed in my heart because, deep down, I never felt like the work and effort to raise funds was the best use of my time. "Shouldn't we be ministering instead of raising funds to minister?" was a question that was always lingering in the back of my mind.

No, I'm not preparing to preach an "anti-fundraising" message to you. I have seen God use the fundraiser to serve successfully in raising money, as well as creating unity, and I'm also aware that some are gifted in this arena and minister with such gifts. When implemented with great planning, preparation and motivated personnel, a fundraiser is a great blessing. And when that fundraiser has a greater agenda attached to it, it can also serve an even greater kingdom purpose. When a fundraiser has an outreach aspect to it, that higher purpose will energize the team with a greater passion.

One question remains, however: "Is fundraising God's first plan of provision for us?" We know, out of personal experience, that God can and will often bless our fundraising efforts. But is it His first choice? Or could it simply be us responding to a financial protocol established by our Western church culture?

One day, during the prep of a very large fundraiser, I was complaining to God about my time spent and asking Him why it just felt wrong. I'm sure you have never done this. But sometimes ministry obligations can get me a little cranky. I was so amazed at the statement the Lord dropped into my heart that I quickly found a pen and wrote it down:

"Fundraising is the church compensating for its disobedience to God."

Wow! It's not that our compensating is inherently wrong. We compensate for many shortcomings in life. Fundraising is not evil, and God can bless it. But how much more of a blessing comes when we tap into a heavenly method?

"You are cursed with a curse, for you are robbing Me, the whole nation of you! [10] *Bring the whole tithe into the storehouse, so that there may be food in My house, and test Me now in this," says the Lord of hosts, "if I will not open for you the windows of heaven and pour out for you a blessing until it overflows.* [11] *Then I will rebuke the devourer for you, so that it will not destroy the fruits of the ground; nor will your vine in the field cast its grapes," says the Lord of hosts (Malachi 3:9-11).*

You might agree that the devourer has not been rebuked from the church both personally and collectively. God set up the financial budget of heaven, a system of sowing and reaping that has never been altered. This concept of giving is a God-designed plan that simply works. The real replacement of the fundraising event is God's people truly trusting Father God in every area of their lives, especially with financial provision.

Recent studies have shown that fewer than 5 percent of American adults tithe (give 10 percent to a church), and this includes all giving. Wow, this includes missions! The Western Christian has a real problem of trust, faith and covetousness.

I recall making my first pastoral house call to a family that our church regularly supplied with food. This single-parent family with four kids was on a very limited budget and, like many families, needed assistance. As I made trips into the house bringing boxes of food and household supplies, I had to keep from stepping on the many pets that were underfoot. The kids were all too eager to tell me the names of these many animals: cats, dogs, hamsters and other cute little critters. They had more than a dozen pets to care for. This family, who had yet to learn the joys of giving to ministry, seemed to be bound by their obligation to feed this zoo of pets.

As the church reviewed its benevolence giving, its leaders decided to educate the receivers of that benevolence, to help avoid the church becoming the main support for pet care. Taking care of widows and orphans is a mandate to the body of Christ. Properly educating them on personal financial management should be part of that mandate as well.

Before your blood starts boiling, let me make this very clear. I have a healthy appreciation for animals. I recognize their place and our connection with them. But contrary to political correctness, I do not believe for a moment that God made any animal to be equal to mankind. If this offends you, I'm very surprised you made it this far in the book.

God designed and created animals to be self-sufficient. We bred and trained them to be human dependent. Stay with me here. I truly enjoy the many benefits these beautiful creatures have added to our quality of life, from police dogs to the snuggle of a pet for that shut-in. And I must also mention the Alaskan Huskies mushing us across the arctic snow. My focus here is not to preach against animals, but rather to bring attention to the area of our financial priorities.

The Associated Press, February 22, 2013:

LOS ANGELES — The U.S. economy may have remained sluggish last year, but Americans refused to scrimp on their pets, with animal lovers spending upwards of $53 billion on food, veterinary care, kennels and other services in 2012.

That's up 5 percent from 2011, when spending first broke the $50 billion barrier, says the American Pet Products Association, a trade group. APPA President and CEO Bob Vetere predicts another 4 percent gain this year. He says spending on services like grooming, boarding, hotels and pet-sitting grew nearly 10 percent during 2012 to almost $4.4 billion.

At about $34.3 billion, food and vet care represented about two-thirds of total spending, with money spent on supplies and over-the-counter medications rising by more than 7 percent. Spending on the growing market of alternative vet care, such as acupuncture, totaled about $12.5 billion.

Acupuncture? Let all of the above sink in for a moment: All the numbers above total $53 BILLION!

A family who would regularly request "sponsorships" for their youth to participate on a missions trip admittedly would spend hundreds a month on pet care. They openly explained the reason they could not give to the church or missions was due to an expensive surgery for an elderly dog. This operation may give the family pet a few more years.

U.S. mission agencies have an annual budget of more than $5.2 billion (*Weber and Welliver* 2007, 13). The average American Christian gives only one penny a day to global missions (Yohannan, *Revolution in World Missions*, 142). These numbers are astonishingly low. Even with the addition of local missions giving, this amount remains a small fraction of what we spend on our pets.

This may help you gain a better perspective. A report on USNews.com disclosed that Americans spent more than $61 billion on their pets in 2011, with the average household spending just more than $500 on their pets during the year. The data shows that pet spending hit a peak in 2008, at $571 per household, then dropped off sharply, eventually hitting $480 in 2010. However, spending on Fluffy and Spot as a share of households' total spending picked up slightly during the recession, from 0.9 percent in 2007 to 1.1 percent during the heart of the downturn in 2008 and 2009.

Labor Department data also shows that Americans remained selflessly devoted to their pets during the recession, holding their spending on pet food steady through the downturn, while cutting back on the luxury of eating out. The data may also signal fatter times ahead for America's pets. Americans aged 55 to 64 spent the most on their pets of any age group, at $636 per year, in 2011. In addition, homeowners spent $653 on average, compared to renters, at $221.

[19]Do not store up for yourselves treasures on earth, where moth and rust destroy, and where thieves break in and steal. [20]But store up for yourselves treasures in heaven, where neither moth nor rust destroys, and where thieves do not break in or steal; [21]for where your treasure is, there your heart will be also (Matthew 6:19-21).

According to Barna Group, which provides research for churches, among others, of the 78 percent-plus of people claiming to be Christian in this country, only about one-third of them are actually showing that lifestyle in some form or fashion. Our pets receive four times more love than the missions and missionaries we support.

[24]Therefore God gave them over in the lusts of their hearts to impurity, so that their bodies would be dishonored among them. [25]For they exchanged the truth

of God for a lie, and worshiped and served the creature rather than the Creator, who is blessed forever. Amen (Romans 1:24-25).

Worship is found in our investments of time and resources. We can unknowingly worship the creatures rather than the Creator if we follow a culture that influences our very beliefs on the value of life. God designed mankind to be dependent on Him. He designed us with ears to hear and a built-in need to hear the good news of the Gospel. If we, the "followers of Jesus," invest more on our pets than on the mission, we have a real problem.

Our investments reveal the motives of our heart.

[24] There is one who scatters, and yet increases all the more, and there is one who withholds what is justly due, and yet it results only in want. [25] The generous man will be prosperous, and he who waters will himself be watered. [26] He who withholds grain, the people will curse him, but blessing will be on the head of him who sells it. [27] He who diligently seeks good seeks favor, but he who seeks evil, evil will come to him. [28] He who trusts in his riches will fall (Proverbs 11:24-28).

Simply put, "the generous man will be prosperous." King David understood who held him up. He knew well that Father God would take care of him, whether he was hiding in a cave or sitting on a throne. And David was a giver in heart and in action.

[23] The steps of a man are established by the Lord, and He delights in his way. [24] When he falls, he will not be

hurled headlong, because the Lord is the One who holds his hand. 25 I have been young and now I am old, yet I have not seen the righteous forsaken or his descendants begging bread. 26 All day long he is gracious and lends, and his descendants are a blessing (Psalm 37:23-26).

There have been many times as I was thinking that God had forsaken me that, out of nowhere, He came through.

It's in these times of need that we have learned the importance of planting seeds for harvest. The saying "you can't out-give God" takes on a real meaning when you put that giving into practice.

It is well with the man who is gracious and lends; he will maintain his cause in judgment (Psalm 112:5).

A great theological debate is attached to the subject of giving. Tithing in particular will stir up tension and blood pressure from both sides of the fence. Whether you support a New Testament giving or an Old Testament tithing belief, the real issue is simply this: There is a real lack of cheerful giving among Christians on the planet.

I will leave the task of diving into this debate to others more qualified. But I will say this: If every follower of Christ who finds it necessary to teach that the concept of giving a tenth is not practiced or promoted in the New Testament was actively giving under the new blood covenant, a covenant that Jesus practiced, then there would be no need to sell another cupcake. Jesus shed all of His blood, symbolizing His sacrificial gift of EVERYTHING for us. Then He called us to take up His cross and follow Him. And He knew this would cost us, cost us everything.

¹For it is superfluous for me to write to you about this ministry to the saints; ²for I know your readiness, of which I boast about you to the Macedonians, namely, that Achaia has been prepared since last year, and your zeal has stirred up most of them. ³But I have sent the brethren, in order that our boasting about you may not be made empty in this case, so that, as I was saying, you may be prepared; ⁴otherwise if any Macedonians come with me and find you unprepared, we — not to speak of you — will be put to shame by this confidence. ⁵So I thought it necessary to urge the brethren that they would go on ahead to you and arrange beforehand your previously promised bountiful gift, so that the same would be ready as a bountiful gift and not affected by covetousness.

⁶Now this I say, he who sows sparingly will also reap sparingly, and he who sows bountifully will also reap bountifully. ⁷Each one must do just as he has purposed in his heart, not grudgingly or under compulsion, for God loves a cheerful giver. ⁸And God is able to make all grace abound to you, so that always having all sufficiency in everything, you may have an abundance for every good deed; ⁹as it is written, "He scattered abroad, He gave to the poor, His righteousness endures forever."

¹⁰Now He who supplies seed to the sower and bread for food will supply and multiply your seed for sowing and increase the harvest of your righteousness; ¹¹you will be enriched in everything for all liberality, which through us is producing thanksgiving to God. [12]For the ministry of this service is not only fully supplying the needs of the saints, but is also overflowing through many thanksgivings to God. [13]Because of the proof given by this ministry, they will glorify God for your obedience to your confession of the Gospel of Christ and for the liberality of your contribution to them and to all, [14]while they also, by prayer on your behalf, yearn for you because of the surpassing grace of God in you. [15]Thanks be to God for His indescribable gift (2 Corinthians 9:1-15).

Let's look again at the sixth verse:

Now this I say, he who **sows sparingly** will also **reap sparingly**, and he who **sows bountifully** will also **reap bountifully**.

To sow, although this speaks metaphorically, its first intent in meaning is literal.

To reap in this verse literally means "to harvest."

The law of sowing and reaping is a fixed law.

We often hear from the pulpit, "God doesn't need your money," and this statement is true. He is not financially strapped. What He desires is much more than your money — it's your heart He wants. You can give your wallet without giving your heart, but you can't give your heart without giving your wallet.

It sure doesn't take much investigative work to find where a person's heart is — just follow the money. A spreadsheet of our personal and business expenditures will read volumes about where our heart is and where we stand in our actual belief of sowing and reaping.

Store up for yourselves treasures in heaven. When a heart is looking toward heaven, then making deposits into that heavenly account will be evident in its daily finances.

For where your treasure is, there your heart will be, also. Find the money, and you find the heart!

[20]*And he said to Him, "Teacher, I have kept all these things from my youth up."* [21]*Looking at him, Jesus felt a love for him and said to him, "One thing you lack: go and sell all you possess and give to the poor, and you will have treasure in heaven; and come, follow Me."* [22]*But at these words he was saddened, and he went away grieving, for he was one who owned much property (Mark 10:20-22).*

From Biblical times to the present, the rich are harder to reach with the Gospel, simply because they have so much more to give up.

The needy are in daily want and desperately need a Savior. But those who live comfortably are prone to be complacent in their hearts. The reality is, the only times I've seen the Lord take away all of the resources from the wealthy is when that person struggled to release their worship of the wealth. This worship of wealth is commonly evident in the Western church, a worshiping of the provision more than the provider. But when we worship the provision rather than the provider, we forfeit the protection.

For because of your trust in your own achievements and treasures, even you yourself will be captured (Jeremiah 48:7).

The early New Testament church understood their

lives were under new management, and they fully trusted Jesus as Lord over "every" area of their life. They had experienced the new freedom and power that came with "letting go" of the resources God placed in their hands and allowing Him to direct those resources to where they needed to go. Their hearts were bent toward heaven, and investing life's treasures into their heavenly account was not a duty, but a desire and a privilege.

[44]*And all those who had believed were together and had all things in common;* [45]*and they began selling their property and possessions and were sharing them with all, as anyone might have need.* [46]*Day by day continuing with one mind in the temple, and breaking bread from house to house, they were taking their meals together with gladness and sincerity of heart (Acts 2:44-46).*

As we learn to live the life of a giver, we will step into new levels of blessing and provision, and that heavenly provision just may come in a unique package.

"Meat" the Need

Provision comes in many ways, and in remote Alaska, you really just can't predict how God will meet the next need.

The camp was low on red meat. Sure, we had plenty of northern pike to eat since they were easy to catch and plentiful. But a fish-only menu had been served for far too long. Then the local traditional chief boated in from the village downriver.

"Do you have a rifle?" he asked, as he joined me for some coffee.

"No," I answered. "Do you have a rifle in camp?" I asked him, and his answer was no as well.

We sat and sipped coffee for a few minutes, and then he said, "Seen a young bull on an island about four miles downriver." I knew we had a legal tag for a bull moose, and our names were on this year's harvest list, but I was really tired from the long summer work days. I was also fully aware of the work that followed pulling the trigger.

"Well, I do have my pistol. Can you get me within 50 yards?" I asked, thinking his answer would be no.

But instead he replied, "I think so."

So a summer intern, Landon, joined me and the chief, and we headed downriver. We circled the island and couldn't find any exit tracks. Convinced that this animal was hidden somewhere in the trees of this 5-acre island, we put our plan into effect.

We dropped Landon off on the south side of the island with a 12-gauge shotgun, loaded with slugs. We told him, "Make lots of noise to flush out the moose to the other side. If you encounter a bear, you know what to do." Something must have moved this bull to this island, and it was highly probable that his motivation was retreating from a bear. We moved the boat to another island to the north with a good vantage point.

After waiting a few minutes, we could see the bull moose moving into the open area. Only packing a handgun, we needed to get close quickly. The chief fired up the boat, and we moved fast to the island. Never taking my eyes off the moose, I could see he was running to the other side of the island. I had little time to make a shot, so I literally made a running leap to the sandy shore as the boat approached it. I ran about 50 yards and stopped at the edge of a wall of brush standing taller than me. When I stopped, so did the moose, and without any sight of him, I started calling. I realized that moose don't normally respond to "calling" in July, but I was hoping to get just enough of his attention that he might move into view.

Well, he did, and I could see the top of his back. I wasn't sure of my distance, but knowing this heavy bullet would drop, I aimed the .44 Mag about three feet over his back and released the bear load. The moose disappeared from view, and after a few minutes, there still was no noise or movement that could be detected. With gun in hand, I slowly made my way toward the moose, not knowing what to expect. After fighting the thick brush, I found him lying dead in the very tracks he had made when I took the shot.

Our summer youth camp enjoyed fresh meat thanks to this provision of God. Sometimes, He sends a package by boat or a delivery by plane, and sometimes He provides massive walking steaks which can only be gathered up through our walk of faith or, in this case, a running faith!

No, I didn't have a big game rifle with me, but I used what I had. After harvesting the moose, we used the range finder to confirm that it was a 74-yard shot, and that bear load was found securely imbedded into the spinal cord of the moose. Within a few hours, we had meat to eat. It would have taken days to order, purchase, freeze and ship meat to this remote camp.

I sure like God's way: all organic, free shipping and He writes the bullet statement.

Chapter Five
Culture Shock

How lovely on the mountains are the feet of him who brings good news, who announces peace and brings good news of happiness, who announces salvation, and says to Zion, "Your God reigns!" (Isaiah 52:7)

Unusual Distractions

The first rule of preaching in bush Alaska is never try to preach a salvation message and hunt bears at the same time. It's just way too distracting.

Let me explain. Most of us who have preached for any length of time have most likely received training on "how to deal with distractions during a service." Well, there are some situations no one can properly prepare you for.

I had given the invitation to come forward for prayer, and dozens of Native teens were responding to a powerful move of God that night, but unfortunately, so were the bears. I say "night," but June in Alaska brings 24-hour sunlight. From the stage of the outdoor gathering area (a tarp-covered roof with no walls), I could clearly see that we had unwanted visitors approaching our camp youth service.

This call to meet Jesus must have been anointed, as these three bears continued approaching our gathering area. Our intercessory/security team was responding to the bears coming from three different directions. These big predators were closing in and were about to change the direction of this service.

Our ministry team, who were serving as prayer support and security for the night, knew that using firearms would be a last resort. For one thing, the words "don't allow any distractions to the service" had been drilled into them by me. They knew that shooting a bear would cause all the kids to turn around and disconnect from what the Holy Spirit was doing in their hearts. Knowing that altar time is the most important time of the entire day's schedule, this interruption simply had to be avoided.

The kids seemed oblivious to the bear drama taking place behind them. I must admit, it was a real challenge for me to continue to pray over youth, lay hands on them and keep the concern from appearing on my face while I watched my staff, literally chasing bears around the camp on foot. The staff did their best to buy us some precious time so we could minister.

For a summer intern from the city, this type of distraction is a major culture shock. In a city outreach or camp you might need security to keep kids from fighting or causing a disturbance or to make sure no firearms make it to the event. In our Alaskan missions endeavors, we train and arm our leaders with firearms to make sure the youth are protected from wild predators. You adapt your ministry methods to work in the culture you are reaching.

Culturally Flexible Without Spiritual Compromise

Staying culturally flexible without becoming spiritually compromised can certainly be a challenge in the field.

Knowing what part of a culture you should support and what parts you shouldn't is not a matter of personal opinion or experience. It's a matter of scriptural comparison.

The Word of God is our foundation and any practice, belief or cultural traditions that counter Biblical standards must not be tolerated. We must be led by the Holy Spirit (as opposed to being led by religious upbringing). You have heard the saying, "Keep the main thing the main thing." In ministry, this is so very true.

I have seen missionaries in the field get upset over cultural practices that make them uncomfortable and then tolerate or even embrace other practices that should never be supported.

For example, there are missionaries who will spend significant effort speaking against the "native drum," yet never confront the alcohol consumed by members of the local church. If they had invested more time into understanding the cultural beliefs, these missionaries would not be moving in fear or misunderstanding.

You see, the native drum is simply a traditional instrument that can be made from local organic materials. Although some shamans have used them in their rituals, these drums were not invented by a shaman. In my field research, I have yet to find Natives who worship these drums. Yet, the worship of TV and sports is obvious in the lives of many ministers who want to rid the Native people of their "evil" drums.

I recall sitting with a well-known Eskimo man at W.E.I.O. (World Eskimo Indian Olympics), where he and I would work together each summer. As we sat to watch the Native dance shows, he would explain the story behind each song and dance. Robert Aiken, known as "Big Bob," a Holy Spirit-filled Eskimo, was not tolerant of any cultural tradition that went against the Word of God.

"See the way they are pointing their arms out and then back in? This dance is a reminder of how the village got a whale during a long period of starvation. It's a celebration and thanks to God for the whale." He would explain the next dance, "This dance is not a good one. It came from the shaman and brings bad power."

Dance after dance, year after year, this man would help me see past my cultural misunderstanding. We have a historical tendency to cover everything we don't understand or find uncomfortable with the same blanket of evil. It's human nature to stand against and eventually kill anything we fear or, for lack of information, can't seem to grasp.

In the '60s and '70s, I caught, raised and sold snakes. I sold them to pet stores and people with gardens. As a kid, I read every book on reptiles and had a solid knowledge of these critters. There wasn't a teacher in my school who knew more than I did about snakes, and I must say my "show and tell" presentations kept the kids on the edge of their seats!

One Friday in seventh grade, I released a 6-foot-2-inch gopher snake named Stanley during one of my reptile presentations. The once-boring classroom became quite lively in a short amount of time. This was a great time to explain, "Less than 3 percent of all snakes on the planet are poisonous, and this gopher snake, also called the bullhead in other states, has no poison. He is a constrictor and must crush his prey before swallowing." But thanks to all that jumping, running and screaming, I'm not sure if they were really grasping the information of my oral report.

The uneducated in the mission field will make decisions out of fear. They will assume all snakes are deadly and should be killed. What they don't know is that the very species of snake they cut the head off of would have removed every gopher from their precious garden. Whether we come against an entire culture or fully embrace the entire culture, we will find ourselves in a place of great compromise.

Much can be researched before you ever enter a given mission field, but the most powerful and enlightening understanding of a culture and its practices is found in relationship with those people. Many things simply can't be learned by Googling.

When I sit with an elder of a tribe, clan or region, I will respectfully ask them questions about their beliefs. "I understand you do such and such; can you tell me the history behind that practice?" Asking them how something started and what purpose it serves to the people are common questions I use in the field. Learning the fundamental beliefs and ancient back story help bring confirmation to what the Spirit of God is showing you.

When we throw the "evil blanket" over a culture, we offend the people and inhibit our chances of creating influence. Likewise, when we fully embrace a culture, we lose sight of our own purpose and find ourselves operating in compromise.

"To be missional, we must learn how to reframe our life, actions and speech in a way that is relevant to those who have not developed a grasp of such highly developed paradigms of culture" (Alton Garrison).

Dinner Thief

It was 4 a.m., and I was awakened from a deep sleep in my tent by the sound of gunfire. As I sat up in bed, it certainly sounded like the cracking of a .22 rifle across the river. I thought to myself, *Who would be up this early, firing a rifle? Not a local I know would be out here, and my team had worked hard until midnight. I'm sure they are dead asleep.* I would have detected a boat coming upriver, as I strategically planted my tent next to the riverbank.

The shots continued to echo across the water, and then the light bulb came on. That's not gunfire! That's the sound of boards breaking!

We had just finished hanging salmon in the smokehouse the day before, and that is where this echoing sound was coming from. Wearing only long johns, work boots, t-shirt and a gun belt, I ran toward the smokehouse about 100 yards downriver. My sloppy approach scared off the predator, and I could hear it running off into the woods. Several boards that made up the outer walls were torn off and broken in half. The breaking of these boards was obviously the "rifle sound" that had cracked on the water. The massive amount of damage this bear had achieved was amazing.

After a quick assessment of the smokehouse and the rest of the camp, I decided to get back to my tent before a team member caught me in my underwear. Before settling in, however, I decided to get a little more prepared this time. Fully dressed with gun belt and boots on, I attempted what would be a short nap.

Snap! Crack! Pow! The sounds began to echo up the river again. But this time I was ready. I moved with stealth and under cover as I approached the smokehouse. My heart was pumping hard, and the view of salmon spread all over the ground only got my temperature up. As I stood inside the cover of our outdoor camp kitchen, I had a good view of the smokehouse and could hear the animal having a feast on the inside.

Before I could gather my thoughts and control my now heavy breathing, he poked his head out of the doorway. I quickly sent a bear load in his direction, and it gracefully flew only inches over his head. He didn't jump or even move his position. He did turn to look downriver, like he was curious about that bullet slashing on the water. This gave me a moment to actually slap myself in the face, rub some sleep from my eyes and regroup for another shot.

He moved just enough to expose his chest, which was all I needed from this big ol' bear at the moment. With much more focus and mental control, I slowly pulled the trigger of my .44 Magnum, sending the massive bear slug into his chest and shoulder. He darted straight for me, and my next round hit him hard, turning him the other direction. These bears can move 35 miles per hour, and I'm convinced he moved much faster than that. He dropped on the trail only 25 yards from his damaging work.

This old black bear was by far the largest I had ever encountered. His face carried the many scars of past battles. His body was also war-ridden with evidence of a hard life. Some fish was salvaged, the walls were repaired and black bear backstrap was on the menu.

Yes, I know what you might be thinking. "This is a youth camp?" Yes, it is. And each missions ministry endeavor will need to properly deal with its cultural influence and environment. While working at other camps, I remember taking shifts with other leaders to guard the snack shack from some overzealous inner-city kids.

The big concern in those camp staff meetings was, "Who got into the Hershey bars last night?" or discussing the "emotional drama over a boy with the junior high girls in cabin four." In our remote youth camps, we actually have staff who stay up all night on bear watch. This is a necessary security measure in these regions. It's part of our ministry culture.

The ability to properly adapt to a cultural lifestyle does not necessarily come with experience in the field. On the contrary, I have seen many seasoned missionaries come to the point where they think they have "done their time" and no longer need to put up with discomfort. It's actually a heart condition rather than notches on a belt. If we lose the sense of privilege to be sent to the field, we risk the chance of it becoming about us and our needs. Your mission should be enjoyable and filled with joy but rarely comfortable.

Sometimes It Stinks

The cold ocean wind brought the temperature down to a biting -35 degrees. We were geared up for the cold but not ready for the painfully penetrating wind. The island was mostly made up of volcanic rock. It was covered in grass in the summer, and this treeless place offered little cover from the winter winds. The church where we were staying greeted us with frozen water pipes and wet carpet from flooding. No working showers was not a real surprise for this team of 16, but the lack of having actual toilets would soon become a challenge.

We had shipped our food in bulk, two weeks prior to our arrival, giving plenty of time for it to arrive in the village before we did. St. Lawrence Island has only two villages, and we planned to have large supplies of food awaiting us in each village. We knew that purchasing food for a team of 16 in these remote areas would be costly, if possible at all. We had spent all of our mission budget on food, supplies and flights. So our food shipments were a great necessity.

After a full day of flying over rugged Alaskan wilderness, we were tired, hungry and really happy to be greeted at the airport by locals who would taxi us on snow machines to the church building where we would be staying. All that was left to do was to locate the containers with our food supply and we would feed this hungry team. Then we could get started with the outreach schedule. I love it when a plan comes together!

St. Lawrence Island is inhabited by strong and resourceful indigenous people. These Inuit Siberian Yup'ik Eskimo people are a whaling community, and they enjoy the delicacy of muktuk. After our arrival at the church, we quickly became aware that our food supply had not arrived. After some investigative phone calls, we were informed that the containers of food were secure in a warehouse across the Bering Sea. Not sure if you caught that … that's 165 miles of frozen ocean between us and food! It would be several days until we would see familiar food, and we were going to have to make do until then.

We were told to make use of any food we could find in the pantry of this uninhabited church. What a blessing to find pancake mix, peanut butter and popcorn. The word circulated through the village that the missionaries were waiting on their food supply. So Eskimo manna was also on the daily menu. Yes, we added muktuk to our wonderful selection of foods. The pancake mix lasted only a short time, but the muktuk was plentiful. If you have not had the pleasure of experiencing this indigenous delicacy, muktuk is whale blubber. To the outsider, it can be an acquired taste. Some adapt to it more easily than others.

Muktuk

> **muk·tuk:** the blubber and skin of a whale when eaten as a food, raw or cooked

"Really? You think I'm gonna eat that? I don't think so," is a statement heard too often in the mission fields of the North. If you are actually allergic to this food and the swelling of your esophagus will kill you, then kindly decline with the explanation of your medical condition. If you are ministering in a country where they ceremonially drink blood and they offer it to you, you can stand on strong Biblical foundations that restrict you from accepting their offer. But if you just don't like the taste of fish? It tastes too fishy to you? Get over your self-focused issues, and eat the blubber!

Placing preferences over principles undermines your purpose.

Never risk offending a people simply because you don't like something. One of the powerful ways to honor someone is to eat what he eats. It represents his way of life and his history. Do I like muktuk? Well, it's not my favorite. But when I'm on Eskimo turf, I eat up, knowing that the very act of doing so can bring honor and healing to those offering it.

Be careful that your "preferences" never take priority over Biblical principles. So you don't like muktuk? Just smile and eat it. You might learn to like it.

Remember how we were without running water and flushing toilets? We did what many locals still do today, shared "honey buckets." No, it's not something you throw a Winnie the Pooh party with. This kind of poo stifles any party.

Honey buckets are actually common in many remote and rural parts of Alaska. You line the inside of the bucket with a plastic bag, then fit the top with a toilet seat lid. These buckets become your temporary toilets.

It's not so bad, not for anyone with a little missionary work under his or her belt. I'm told that the name "honey bucket" came from actual buckets that were once used as containers for honey. But I have found you will commonly hear the statement, "Honey, can you take out the bucket?"

When you take a team into an arctic winter situation

with no flushing water and then feed them a constant diet of pancakes, peanut butter, popcorn and muktuk, well, need I tell you just how quickly those 5-gallon plastic buckets can fill up?

Within days, most of our team was suffering from some stage of diarrhea and/or early flu symptoms, which, as you might imagine, kept our buckets filling up faster than the norm. It was late into the night, with outside temperatures of -35 degrees, but the buckets needed to be transported to the dump. We had no idea where the dump was located. All I knew was that we needed this aroma out of the building and the buckets returned empty fast!

One of my interns and another young man were chosen for this sensitive mission. One walked in front to navigate in the dark with an undersized flashlight, hoping to find a local to show the right direction to the dump. They would later find a local who would inform them, "No one goes to the dump at night. The polar bears are out at night, and it's dangerous!"

On their way to the dump, the young man walking with one full bucket in each hand lost his footing in the snow. As he recalled the events later, he said that both buckets fell quickly to the ground, and on impact the contents of each bucket sloshed up and out, splattering his body from head to toe. Yes, with the DNA deposits of his fellow missions team.

I heard a pounding on the door. *What took them so long?* I was thinking, as I headed to the church door. Upon opening it, I was truly amazed at what I saw. Never had I seen anyone in such a nasty predicament. Not only was the poor guy covered in poo, the human glaze of nastiness had frozen solid on impact. He was a standing poop-sicle! He tried to explain, but his discolored face was frozen in a painfully hideous display that could only leak groans and mumbles.

Hopefully, you won't need to deal with a human poop-sicle on your next mission. But chances are you will be challenged by the environment and local culture and customs.

Learn the people before you go. Take time to research their history. Prepare your team to honor the people by eating the traditional foods served. It is easy to dishonor in the name of ministry. Make sure the principles conquer your preferences.

Chapter Six
The Lead Trip

*"I will send My messenger, who will prepare the way
before Me. Then suddenly the Lord you are seeking will
come to His temple; the messenger of the covenant,
whom you desire, will come," says the Lord Almighty.*
(Malachi 3:1)

51 Below Zero

The runway lights off in the distance broke through
the dark cold flight. The temperature in this remote village
that we were about to land in was -51 degrees. What I
thought was freezing cold inside the plane was actually
warm compared to what we would soon encounter.

The flight assistant, who I would guess was not paid
enough to care, proceeded to throw our new JBL speakers
from the plane to the hard icy ground. I moved rather
quickly considering the arctic slap in the face and caught

the second speaker before it joined the first one on the ice.

One of the local dog mushers walked over to the plane and said, "Hey, Pastor, ready for a dog run? I'm taking the dogs for a short ride, 'bout 40 miles."

I was trying to wrap that idea around my frozen brain. My hands were numb, my eyelashes were sticking to my face, the wind was cutting through my winter gear and the recorded 51 below zero was feeling much colder than that. "Not this time, but thank you for the offer" should have been my response. But I recall saying, "What?! Are you trying to kill me on my first day here? Ask me again when it warms up to zero."

He smiled and said, "Zero is too hot for the dogs; they overheat and can't run as far."

While loading the speakers, I was thinking, *What animal or person could possibly prefer -51 degrees and purposely go out into it? Don't they know that that is actually 84 degrees below freezing?!* Hypothermia occurs when the core temperature of the human body falls below 95 degrees. Well, if that's true, I'm sure I hit well below that mark before I stepped off the plane.

Transportation for this large team traveling with me was a real challenge. After the arrival of an old pickup truck, a snow machine and a very old school bus to the gravel airport, we were able to get our team and all the bulky gear to a building on the other side of the village that would house us for this outreach.

The school gym, often the only village facility that we can use in the winter, was to be our ministry location for the next several days. There were logistics to work out, people to find and meet, sound equipment to set up and worship services to prepare, all without a vehicle to assist.

The mile-and-a-half walk to the gym would be deadly without the proper winter gear. So "hurry up and wait" would be the process for each forward step on this mission trip. Yes, ministry took place, but the logistics sure could have gone smoother. My lead trip for this outreach had taken place in the summer, and we were going in the dead of winter, not the most optimal to say the least.

The lead trip is the most underestimated ingredient to a successful mission experience. There is a good reason that the military will not engage in any conflict, rescue, invasion or maneuver without first gathering all the information they can obtain from the field. Collection of intelligence becomes invaluable and helps formulate their methods to better reach the intended goals of that mission. A lead trip to that village in the winter, under those same conditions, would have greatly improved the logistics of that mission and given us more time to minister and with less time spent on improvising.

One of our annual outreaches involves traveling the Yukon River. After the first year of this boat tour to villages, it became very evident that we spent far too much time coordinating the ministry rather than doing the ministry. Taking some tips from the military model, I formed a small team of three to four people that we called the RECON TEAM. This team was not selected randomly. On the contrary, I selected people who had particular gifts to fit the recon mission. They were not only gifted for their part in recon, but also able to work well together as a team. They would fly by private plane into each village two or three days prior to the rest of the team arriving. Their mission consisted of several objectives:

- make contact with the local village leaders
- confirm proper permissions
- establish the necessary relational connections
- assess the needs of the people
- investigate recent events, deaths, suicides, accidents, etc.
- find housing and/or camping area for the coming team
- clear land for the team tents, if necessary
- find tools and/or extra equipment needed to prep housing area
- find drinking water access
- locate public showers and restrooms, if available
- investigate the local event schedule
- draft a village map and plan for logistics
- arrange transportation of team and equipment
- schedule and/or confirm services and events
- draft a ministry schedule for the team
- hang posters, walk the village and promote the events
- generate momentum for the arriving team
- spiritually assess the focused warfare on the village

- prayer walks, interceding over the local people
- overall prepare the way for the team

Most often when we engage in a lead trip, it takes place far in advance of the actual mission. These recon team assignments serve a valuable purpose a few days prior to our collective mission. Much like John the Baptist, the recon team paves the way for ministry success.

re·con·nais·sance
1. The act of reconnoitering
2. Military: a search made for useful military information in the field, especially by examining the ground
3. Surveying, Civil Engineering: a general examination or survey of a region, usually followed by a detailed survey
4. Geology: an examination or survey of the general geological characteristics of a region

re·con·noi·ter
1. Inspect, observe or survey (the enemy, the enemy's strength or position, a region, etc.) in order to gain information for military purposes
2. Examine or survey (a region, area, etc.) for engineering, geological or other purposes

The reconnaissance team described above is one aspect of the lead trip concept, a process that, if practiced, will save you valuable time and money in the field. One of its greatest benefits is the gathering of intel on the lead trip far in advance of the actual mission. These lead trips can literally steer the direction and the mission, strongly influencing the methods for greater effectiveness in the field. Similar to the recon objectives mentioned earlier, the intentions of the lead trip will take on a greater depth.

Spiritual Mapping

I won't spend a great amount of time on this subject, but let me attempt to bring some clarity to the concept. You will find strong beliefs on both sides of the fence on this subject, with compelling justification to support either stance.

Some say ministry, especially mission work, will be completely ineffective without spiritual mapping, while others will tell you that the very concept is misguided and demonically influenced. I believe both views have swung the pendulum a bit too far, in opposite directions. Anytime we make a "system" from a concept, develop it into a doctrine and then revolve our mission around it, we step onto unstable ground.

18And Jesus came up and spoke to them, saying, "All authority has been given to Me in heaven and on earth. 19Go therefore and make disciples of all the nations, baptizing them in the name of the Father and the Son and the Holy Spirit (Matthew 28:18-19).

Let me clarify. Jesus told us that He was given "all authority" in heaven and on earth. It's not about being fearful of what has/is taking place on the land: Jesus gave us that authority. Moses served a God of power and real miracles, yet Father God gave him the wisdom to send in spies to look over the land.

¹Then the Lord spoke to Moses saying, ²"Send out for yourself men so that they may spy out the land of Canaan, which I am going to give to the sons of Israel; you shall send a man from each of their fathers' tribes, everyone a leader among them." ³So Moses sent them from the wilderness of Paran at the command of the Lord, all of them men who were heads of the sons of Israel. ⁴These then were their names: from the tribe of Reuben, Shammua the son of Zaccur; ⁵from the tribe of Simeon, Shaphat the son of Hori; ⁶from the tribe of Judah, Caleb the son of Jephunneh; ⁷from the tribe of Issachar, Igal the son of Joseph; ⁸from the tribe of Ephraim, Hoshea the son of Nun; ⁹from the tribe of Benjamin, Palti the son of Raphu; ¹⁰from the tribe of Zebulun, Gaddiel the son of Sodi; ¹¹from the tribe of Manasseh (a tribe of Joseph), Gaddi the son of Susi; ¹²from the tribe of Dan, Ammiel the son of Gemalli; ¹³from the tribe of Asher, Sethur the son of Michael; ¹⁴from the tribe of Naphtali, Nahbi the son of Vophsi; ¹⁵from the tribe of Gad, Geuel the son of Machi. ¹⁶These are the names of the men whom Moses sent to spy out the land; but Moses called Hoshea the son of Nun, Joshua.

¹⁷When Moses sent them to spy out the land of Canaan, he said to them, "Go up there into the Negev; then go up into the hill country. ¹⁸See what the land is like, and whether the people who live in it are strong or weak, whether they are few or many. *¹⁹How is the land in which they live, is it good or bad? And how are the cities in which they live, are they like open camps or with fortifications? ²⁰How is the land, is it fat or lean? Are there trees in it or not? Make an effort then to get some of the fruit of the land." Now the time was the time of the first ripe grapes.*

²¹So they went up and spied out the land from the wilderness of Zin as far as Rehob, at Lebo-hamath. ²²When they had gone up into the Negev, they came to Hebron where Ahiman, Sheshai and Talmai, the descendants of Anak, were. (Now Hebron was built seven years before Zoan in Egypt.)

²³Then they came to the valley of Eshcol and from there cut down a branch with a single cluster of grapes; and they carried it on a pole between two men, with some of the pomegranates and the figs. ²⁴That place was called the valley of Eshcol, because of the cluster which the sons of Israel cut down from there (Numbers 13:1-24).

The "Lead Trip Team Report" will differ depending on who you send. In most cases the lead trip or recon will not take 40 days, but however long it takes, the accuracy of that report comes down to who gives it.

Shammua, Shaphat, Caleb, Igal, Hoshea (Joshua), Palti, Gaddiel, Gaddi, Ammiel, Sethur, Nahbi and Geuel were the 12 men sent to spy out the land. Of these 12, there were two who could see through the eyes of the Lord, and their report was immersed in faith.

²⁵When they returned from spying out the land, at the end of forty days, ²⁶they proceeded to come to Moses and Aaron and to all the congregation of the sons of Israel in the wilderness of Paran, at Kadesh; and they brought back word to them and to all the congregation and showed them the fruit of the land. ²⁷Thus they told him, and said, "We went in to the land where you sent us; and it certainly does flow with milk and honey, and this is its fruit. ²⁸Nevertheless, the people who live in the land are strong, and the cities are fortified and very large; and moreover, we saw the descendants of Anak there. ²⁹Amalek is living in the land of the Negev and the Hittites and the Jebusites and the Amorites are living in the hill country, and the Canaanites are living by the sea and by the side of the Jordan."

³⁰Then Caleb quieted the people before Moses and said, "We should by all means go up and take possession of it, for we will surely overcome it." ³¹But the men who had gone up with him said, "We are not able to go up against the people, for they are too strong for us." ³²So they gave out to the sons of Israel a bad report of the land which they had spied out, saying, "The land through which we have gone, in spying it out, is a land that devours its inhabitants; and all the people whom we saw in it are men of great size. ³³There also we saw the Nephilim (the sons of Anak are part of the Nephilim); and we became like grasshoppers in our own sight, and so we were in their sight" (Numbers 13:25-33).

When God's people see what God sees and respond with faith, their promotion is inevitable.

Using methods of spiritual mapping in the lead trip will strengthen your missions outreach with clarity and confirmation of your mission goals.

The process of gaining spiritual history is a wise move that can help direct your prayer and missions focus. It's not about knowing "everything" before boots hit the ground. But going to the field knowing "nothing" has stifled our forward movement in missions far too long.

Too often, I have watched well-meaning missionaries and/or teams march into a culture and attempt to bulldoze their mission agenda onto that community. When they encounter resistance (and they usually do), they then blame it on the enemy, the people's hardened hearts or the community's coldness to the Gospel. Spiritual mapping is simply the recon of spiritual history. Learning where a people came from, where they are today and where they are headed is wisdom in action.

The foundational focus behind spiritual mapping can be found in these three words: prayer, revelation and research.

Prayer

As covered in Chapter Three, prayer is necessary for mission success. The lead trip can give you relevant information that will help direct your prayers with accuracy. This informed intercession will pay great dividends in your mission prep and planning.

Revelation

All revelation must line up with the Word of God. On location, God has an opportunity to reveal and confirm things clearly to us from that authentic vantage point.

Research

We were designed to learn from our history. That was a major reason that God wanted Israel to "remember" their history. The mission fields that you are going to have unique historical information that will help you take them to the next level.

One of the main purposes of spiritual mapping should be to gain a heavenly perspective. If we can better see the people and their needs through the eyes of God, we bypass much wasted time. We can then focus our ministry in the direction most effective to reach that people group.

The intent of this mapping research should never be focused on hunting down demons, but rather on exposing the wounded areas of a people and bringing healing to those lives. Here are a few questions that, if answered, could be very helpful in aligning your mission with the leading of the Holy Spirit:

- How was the land acquired?
- What significant wars or battles took place on that land?
- How was the village, city or town established?
- What is the relational history among different ethnicities?

- What is the economic condition?
- What is the cultural history?
- What religious or political institutions have dominated the culture?
- What Christian history does it have?
- Have there been broken covenants or lost trust?
- Is witchcraft a part of their culture?
- What is the population and average age of that city, village or region?
- What is the cost of living and estimated cost of supplies on location?
- What resources will be needed and/or effective in this culture?
- What are the needs of the local missionaries?
- How should we best enter a village, town, city or people group with the Gospel?

You might rethink bringing your usual Vacation Bible School material after learning that the governmental leadership emerged from greed, lying, murder, theft and rebellion and was financed by prostitution and drug manufacturing. How we go about bringing the Good News of Jesus should be influenced by the needs and condition of the people we want to reach.

Preparing the Lead Trip Team

As mentioned for the recon team, don't just send those who want to go on the lead trip. Be strategic in your selection.

THE LEAD TRIP

Much like assembling the "A-Team," I attempt to send those who have a particular skill that will maximize the effectiveness of the lead trip. The size of your lead trip team may depend on your budget and your available personnel. Both often come into play, and considering that most churches, ministries and organizations don't have a budget set aside for the lead trip, making the very best use of those resources will help confirm the need for this budget in the future.

It has become our policy to refrain from sending someone alone. Two to four people who have the A-Team skills to accomplish the recon mission is our goal.

Here is a list of qualities to look for when selecting your team:

1) Send the Visionaries

36As for the men whom Moses sent to spy out the land and who returned and made all the congregation grumble against him by bringing out a bad report concerning the land, 37even those men who brought out the very bad report of the land died by a plague before the Lord. 38But Joshua the son of Nun and Caleb the son of Jephunneh remained alive out of those men who went to spy out the land (Numbers 14:36-38).

It was visionaries who brought back a positive report to Moses. In junior high, getting a bad report card was a painful proposition. In the arena of faith, giving a bad report card is harmful to your health. Those with vision can see through their faith, as well as with their eyes. They see perspectives that the Holy Spirit is highlighting for them, and they see perspectives that those consumed with self-preservation and/or doubt have trouble recognizing.

2) Send the Honoring

People who naturally serve others will naturally honor others. If they have a high standard of comfort, honoring others will be a challenge for them. Send low-maintenance people, those who don't need to be catered to, but those looking to serve.

3) Send the Detailed

Select those with an eye for detail. Those who take detailed notes of information and conversations. The people who notice the bag that got left on the seat of the plane by others. These are the kind of people who actually think that little things matter, like checking the fuel gauge before driving off. They refuse to operate on assumption and make sure the flight has no last-minute gate changes.

4) Send the Videographer

Obtaining video or digital memory of the lead trip will be a great benefit in the debriefing report. You may not find this person in the picture, but they will log the entire team and its findings throughout the recon. Capturing these images will be invaluable when it comes time to prepare promotional materials.

5) Send the Relational

Look for people who easily connect with others. People with true relational skills can win people over with their smile. These people are flexible in relationships and not easily derailed. They unite the rest of the team through their love and concern of others.

6) Send the Intercessor

A person focused on prayer will pave the way for the team. Yes, the entire team should be people of prayer. But there are those gifted in this area, and they will often spur the team to pray. While others are busy interacting, the intercessor will commonly be found in the back praying intently for the team and God's direction.

7) Send the Confident

Choose a person who is emotionally strong. A secure personality, who can keep the team safe, both emotionally and physically. A person who can keep the team focused in times of challenge is a leader.

Okay, I know what you are thinking, and, yes, a lead team of seven just might be overkill. More importantly, it would not be practical. Thankfully you and those you work with are blessed with more than one gift. In your lead team selection, try to find people who fulfill several of these gifts, talents and abilities. I have been blessed over the years to train up people who can operate in most of the areas mentioned.

For example, if I am designing a team of three, I would first look for a leader who can also overlap in two or more of the areas mentioned. Maybe this person can lead with <u>confidence</u> and also be a <u>visionary</u> who loves to <u>honor</u> others.

Another member might first serve as the <u>intercessor</u>, but also is gifted in <u>relational</u> people skills. The third member of this team might be great in <u>photography</u> and a master of <u>detail</u>.

Could a war be fought and won without the recon doing its job? I'm sure it could, but I'm convinced it would take longer, cost more and work the team harder rather than smarter. The military knows that with the proper intelligence, the preparation for a mission will be maximized, and its team will enter the mission with a greater confidence when their boots hit the ground.

Confirm Your Mission

In Joshua 6, the two men who had successfully returned with a full report from their reconnaissance to the city of Jericho were given an order: *Joshua said to the two men who had spied out the land, "Go into the harlot's house and bring the woman and all she has out of there, as you have sworn to her."*

It's not enough to move forward with a good missions idea: Confirm that it is a God idea. If you know you heard the voice of the Lord, then set your face like flint (Isaiah 50:7) and move forward. Forward in faith, strength and courage, but not without wisdom in operation.

Another important part of qualifying the mission is investigating the integrity of the mission field and/or the local missionary you intend to work with.

For every legitimate mission project, there seem to be two counterfeits. The number of churches and houses that receive monthly coats of paint and refurnishing is alarming. Buildings that were later sold for prostitution, fake orphanages that paid the pockets of a few, and the list goes on and on. Like me, just maybe you have received those countless e-mails from Africa, India, Afghanistan, South America, etc., asking for a team to join their ministry that has built hundreds of orphanages and is reaching tens of thousands, yet they need your team and your resources. Because this takes place at such a high rate, there are some who would strongly advise you to "cancel" that short-term mission! On the contrary, we must be much more proactive in reaching the lost in every mission field, but wisdom calls for research, background and confirming.

Voice in the Storm

Only 20 miles from the village, and I was determined to get us there. It was dark, and the wind was blowing viciously, adding to the -35-degree temperatures. Visibility was minimal, and the snowdrifts covered up the road so much that I was using trees as landmarks to keep us on the road. With the high beams on, it was a total whiteout, so low beams, low gear and four-wheel drive were in order.

The massive powder drifts we were powering through were more than three feet deep now, and every impact temporarily blinded us completely.

As we crested a mountain, our dim lights revealed a sea of snow ahead. Not being able to decipher where the road was under the wall of snow, I was forced to stop the truck. Grabbing a mag light and gearing up with all the apparel I could wear, I stepped into the storm to investigate the road ahead. Fighting the wind, I made my way farther into the snow. About 10 yards from the truck, I bumped my shin on something hard. Pushing away the snow revealed a flatbed trailer, which had been abandoned in the middle of the road. *Wow,* I thought, *someone must have needed to drop that thing behind him just to get through.*

I climbed on top of it to get a better look with the flashlight to see just how far this drift covered the road. Wait, what's that? There was the other part of the story: a full-sized pickup truck, empty but half covered in snow, about 20 yards from the trailer. Just as I was formulating a plan to get past these roadblocks, I heard the voice of the Lord loud and clear, "Go back now!" Deep in thought, I was plotting my intended path to get through and ignored this first request. We had a mission! We had ministry to do, and we didn't come this far to give up. So I was thinking as I heard that voice again, "Go back now!" This was much louder and resonated over the noise of the wind.

I turned and started toward our truck. As I

approached, I could see that the snowdrifts were climbing up the truck, and in those short minutes, the snow was already at the top of the tires. My aggressive walking to the truck changed to running as I heard, "Go back now!" for the third and final time.

Getting into the truck, I looked behind me to see that the snowdrift we had just punched through was not only now completely recovered with snow, but much deeper. "Hang on!" were my words to the team as we bulldozed with full power in reverse, up the mountain!

We busted through drift after drift for more than 300 yards, in reverse, until I could find a place to turn around. As we crested the top of the hill, I stopped and attempted to make a call with my cell phone. I had never tried a connection that far from town, but I felt an urgency to give it a shot. To my surprise, the phone rang! The connection was just long enough to tell my wife we were aborting the mission and heading home.

Hearing the voice of the Lord is imperative to the success of a mission, but responding to that voice is equally important. The real lesson here is not found in my example of hearing the voice of the Holy Spirit in the field. The real lesson can be found in my *not* listening to that same voice before we headed on this ministry mission. It is the hearing and obeying of God's voice that secures a mission's success.

Was I ready to preach and reach the lost? Oh, yes! Ready and willing to move forcefully ahead! But a call to the State Weather Hotline or to the Troopers for Highway

Reports or maybe a call to the village before I headed out just might have saved time and resources. If only I had taken a moment to respond to that familiar voice of the Holy Spirit before I drove us into the storm.

Hearing the voice of the Lord in the middle of the storm is vital to the success of the mission, but hearing His voice *prior* to the storm can provide enlightening insight for your missions quest.

If the lead trip is the most underestimated ingredient in a successful mission experience, then it's time to activate this process and enjoy its many benefits. You can win the battle and the war.

CHAPTER SEVEN
UNITED PURPOSE

¹Therefore I, the prisoner of the Lord, implore you to walk in a manner worthy of the calling with which you have been called, ²with all humility and gentleness, with patience, showing tolerance for one another in love, ³being diligent to preserve the unity of the Spirit in the bond of peace. ⁴There is one body and one Spirit, just as also you were called in one hope of your calling; ⁵one Lord, one faith, one baptism, ⁶one God and Father of all who is over all and through all and in all.
(Ephesians 4:1-6)

Storm Island

"Did you tie off the boats?" I asked a young man on our team. He said that he had. I persisted and asked, "Did you secure them solidly to the ground? I think this storm will only get worse during the night." He went to double check before we all climbed into our tents.

The wind and rain were pounding the tent wall with such force that we took turns holding up the frame from the inside to keep our summer condos from collapsing. Hours later, the storm was still raging. Concerned for our boats, I yelled to the other tent at the top of my voice, "Go double check the boat ropes!"

A few minutes later I would hear a statement that would send chills up my spine. "How many boats do we have?"

He was running toward my tent and yelling this question. He knew the answer, but was somehow hoping that I would give him a smaller number than what he remembered securing to the shore. "Three! We have three boats!"

Throwing on my pants, boots and gun belt, I ran out into the storm toward the riverbank. Sure enough, only two boats could be seen tied to the shore. After a quick inspection, it was clear that the tree the third boat was attached to had been dragged away.

There was no sign of a boat downriver. No time for forensics — we had a boat to find. Of all the boats to break loose on the mighty Yukon, don't you know it had to be the new jet boat. Not just the brand-new boat, but the boat on which we chose to store more than 300 gallons of boat fuel!

I don't recall ever making a faster boat launch. Three of us were in the other jet boat and heading downriver at record speed. We fuel up and check the oil of each boat at every stop. That way, our boats are ready to go in the case of an emergency like this. Well, this was one of those times you appreciate good maintenance habits. Procrastinating the boat prep when we landed would have secured our failure to rescue the craft for sure.

In my haste, I broke every personal boating rule: no life vest, no GPS, no two-way radio. Moreover, I was feeling the pain of not having my goggles to protect my eyes. The rain felt like I was being pelted with shotgun fire as we ran the RPMs to maximum. But utilizing all 200 horsepower was necessary if we were going to find that boat.

Visibility was minimal, and the landscape began to look very confusing. "What is that up ahead?" I was speaking into the wind. What I saw was a wall! Yes, a solid wall of rain like I had never seen before. And it was moving violently toward us.

I thought we were heading into it, but I think it was actually heading into us! It literally looked like a massive wall of water from the river to the top of the cloud line. I'll never forget the impact we experienced when we busted into this dense wall of rain. I was concerned that we would take on so much water we would sink.

As we exited the storm front, I could see something off in the distance. Could it be our lost boat? At about 200 yards, I was sure it was our boat, but it was drifting quickly toward a large cut bank. Not good.

Cut banks are simply the most dangerous spots on a

river. They are where unmeasurable amounts of turbulent water come crashing into a wall of land and get diverted violently. When navigating a boat, the pilot knows to stay a safe distance away from these deathtraps.

Now our lost boat, loaded down with enough fuel to blow up Fort Knox, was not only spinning into a cut bank, but it had no pilot! A plan was quickly put into effect: My associate Jamie would take control of our rescue boat, while I jumped to the drifting craft. It was at that moment that I remembered I was not wearing my life vest.

As the boats made contact, I jumped over and started the motor on our wayward boat as fast as I could. The motor started, and I maneuvered the loaded beast away from certain disaster. I looked behind me to see the water crashing against the cut bank only a boat length away. Wow, that was close!

Jamie led the way back upriver with another teammate, Ross, helping with the navigation. I had trouble keeping up because on top of the heavy load of fuel and the massive amount of rainwater, the boat had also sucked up some debris, making upriver travel painfully slow. It was on this long upriver venture that the absence of a raincoat and headgear dawned on me.

I had left in such a hurry from my tent that proper clothing was not a thought on my mind. Well, it sure was a thought now! The adrenaline that had kept me warm was gone, and I had dropped from emergency mode to survival mode. I could feel the cold from head to toe, and my soaking wet t-shirt offered little thermal assistance.

Although the worst of the storm was now moving upriver from me, visibility was still difficult. I had lost sight of the lead boat and was struggling to find my way. With so many islands, sandbars and channels, I was not clear as to the right direction. The trek downriver was at full throttle. Now my slow speed was working against me. "I should be there by now," I kept saying. No radio, no GPS, no map. And I was shaking violently from the early stages of hypothermia.

Even so, I remained clear-headed enough to know what to do. We keep minimal emergency gear in each boat: a tarp, bottled water, matches, paper, a small container of diesel fuel and an MRE or two. I knew that if I didn't find camp soon, I would need to look for a safe place to dock the boat and build a fire.

Over the years, I've seen the wonderful use of diesel fuel. You can take completely soaked logs and get a roaring fire going. I've used it to save someone from hypothermia more than once. It was while I was combing the shorelines for a safe place to wait out the storm and warm up that I spotted camp.

This camping spot earned the name "Storm Island" and will forever be remembered by me as such. A place of intended rest, it became a place of unexpected stress. To this day, when I ask the question, "Did you secure the boats?" I have a tendency to explain the question with a lot of detail. The words "boat" and "adrift" are two words I intend to never hear in the same sentence again.

Communication is one of our biggest challenges.

Whether it's in the business world or ministry arena, the ability to keep everyone on the same page with clear understanding will forever be a goal. We invest in "communication seminars" and bring in motivational speakers to help bring attention and alignment to this area. We do it because we know unity is highly difficult without it.

A continual barrage of personal, print and electronic messages will help your process of selling a vision and keeping the whole team informed and unified. But my experience is that no matter how much communications teaching you thrust on your team, there will always be that one person who feels out of the loop and under-informed. Just do your best to over-inform the rest.

Miscommunications are most often attributed to "misunderstandings" and "inadequate communications." Let's take a closer look at these two:

Misunderstandings

Misunderstandings are very common and can be the fault of both parties. Continually sending logistics updates, encouragement and prayer focus will help fight misunderstandings with your team. Because I have a tendency to speak in bullet statements, especially in my memos, it has been helpful for me to have people who question my memo to seek clarity for themselves and others. Make sure there is **clarity** in all memos and announcements. Never assume that everyone knows what you are talking about or thinking.

The other side of the misunderstanding falls on the team member. As a member of a missions team, staying informed should be a priority. Always reply to e-mails, memos, etc., with questions for clarity or simply to acknowledge that you received it. If a team member regularly feels out of the loop, it's usually because they are, and they need to look at how the loop works.

Inadequate Communication

This miscommunication usually is the responsibility of leadership. Giving partial information can sometimes be worse than no information at all. Communicating the big picture will help the team gain personal confidence that will lead to collective unity. There have been many times that, in my detailed thinking or processing for a mission event, I thought that I had communicated those details, even though I had not. A written memo will help keep the leader on track and far from assumptions.

With unified purpose, your mission is achievable.

A wonderful byproduct of properly communicating the vision and plan of a mission is a team growing in unity. With every layer of detailed clarity, the team will continue to meld together in spirit and truth. Their like-mindedness will make them stronger mentally, emotionally and spiritually.

Unity is obtainable. But a leader's communication must be constant to fight against the enemy of unity — independence. Independence fights against the very thing that will promote you — unity.

Professional communication is really an essential component of the success of a team's mission. Although spiritual attacks are real, I propose that most organizational problems occurring in the field are a direct result of poor communications, starting from the top.

Here are a few helpful steps that will improve your communicational efforts:

1) Keep a running file of communication.

File your memos, letters, updates and meeting notes. This will help you keep information accurate and chronologically in order.

2) Develop a "two-way" system.

Confirm that the communication is working on the other end by training team members to always reply to your e-mails. If they are constantly clear and concise in their reply, you will have a better idea of whether or not they are on the same page. Never *assume* they got the memo, message or meeting information.

3) Return your calls.

Always return a call, even if you don't have the answer they need. "Just got your message. I don't have that info yet, but didn't want to leave you hanging. Please call me again in two days, and I should have that information. Thank you!" That 15 seconds of invested time will pay back great dividends. One more thing I would recommend to a leader is <u>ANSWER YOUR PHONE</u>! It's sad to find out that in the professional arena, ministers are known for their elusive, unprofessional behavior. Make sure you are not contributing to that reputation.

4) Speak to the team members as individuals.

Be specific in your direction and information. Be accurate. Refrain from "guessing" your way through a memo or meeting. In all correspondence, speak to the person rather than to the group. Personalize your messages. Be real.

5) Schedule adequate meetings.

There is no replacement for a face-to-face encounter. Make the schedule, prep and prayer meetings part of the overall commitment. If someone won't make the group gatherings a priority, then maybe this mission is not best for him or her. Better to have a smaller unified team than a larger dysfunctional one.

Moreover, in physical meetings, make a point to:

- make eye contact
- speak passionately
- use body language
- use gestures
- speak the truth
- speak with clarity
- address the key points
- share encouragement
- show your steps of faith

MISSION ACCOMPLISHED

You can also save valuable time by sending the meeting agenda and needs ahead of time, giving the team time to prep and pray prior to the group meeting. Put more emphasis on the areas of communication that require the most personal contact, i.e.:

1. meetings
2. video conferencing
3. phone calls
4. video messages
5. e-mails
6. social messaging
7. texting

I find it very interesting that the first choice of communication for many just happens to be the lowest form of contact we have available to us, texting.

Yes, there are some people who will potentially walk away from the best of meetings with some confusion and/or misunderstanding, but that potential for confusion increases dramatically from number 1 to 7.

For those mission team members, here is a short list that will help you prepare and do your part to cultivate a spirit of unity:

At-home prayer:
- reply to all communication attempts
- actually read the memos
- keep your notes and memos in a file

- keep a functional calendar (whatever method works for you), and keep track of dates, deadlines and departures
- schedule personal prayer times focusing on the needs of the mission

At-home logistics:
- personally prepare in advance, physically, spiritually, emotionally and financially
- open a missions account to protect your place in the mission
- set up a staging area where you can place each item for packing and check off your list — a table in a room or garage will be helpful for organizing gear and supplies
- Follow through with assignments; read this book

At-missions team meetings:
- come prepared, do your homework
- focus on the speaker and/or leader communicating
- avoid interrupting, be respectful
- avoid criticism; maybe you are more seasoned than the leader, but show your experience through your strength in following
- show your interest; be attentive, don't be looking at your smart phone
- take personal notes; you won't remember everything

- yes, ask questions, but not those tainted with self-motives

Behold, how good and how pleasant it is for brothers to dwell together in unity! (Psalm 133:1).

If we don't communicate, the enemy will.

In communication with the team, the intent of the mission must be made clear. If the purpose of a given outreach or mission trip is simply to fill a gap in the ministry calendar, then true success will be a challenge, and team members will sense the void of vision.

If you call it missions work, than make it about missions.

We as leaders have done an injustice to this generation by candy-coating a missions trip to the point that the taste of candy becomes foremost in their missions memory bank. As we covered "what mission work is" in Chapter One, make sure your ministry event fits and fulfills the title of your event.

If you are promoting it as your "Mission to Mexico" trip, but the magnet that pulls them in to fill the bus seats is Six Flags, Disneyland and all the shopping, then you have just reinforced the idea that they must be entertained to do ministry.

This spirit of entertainment that our Western culture pushes into their thinking now has been validated in their view of missions. If we can't separate ourselves from self-gratification for even a short-term missions trip, then much ministry, as well as opportunity to personally and collectively grow, will be lost. Make sure your missions team is focused on the mission.

I recall, in the early '80s, making numerous phone calls to pastors in remote communities. My desire was to give youth some hands-on encounters with home missions at an entry level of serving. I knew that if I could spend the time training them, we could be a great encouragement and blessing to the pastors and congregations of smaller communities.

In response to these calls, I would hear many different versions of the same story:

"We had a youth group come in for a week last summer. My wife and I are still cleaning up the mess and putting out the fires they started."

"No, thank you, never again. It took us four months to catch up on the electric bill, and my wife got a part-time job just to pay for replenishing all the paper products."

"Do you have any idea how much my wife and I spent to feed that team? We can hardly feed our own family, and many in this small town are out of work."

"Last time I said yes to a youth missions team, we had to replace a $300 microphone, repair a doorframe and replace a window. No, thanks."

The responses were overwhelming. I was amazed at the personal stories and, frankly, embarrassed to call myself a youth pastor as each call ended. I remember apologizing to each pastor for the actions, or non-actions, of other leaders and teams abusing the name of missions, outreach, ministry and, overall, the name of Jesus. So many ministers had been burned in the name of missions that they had closed their hearts to it.

Here was the predicament: The ministers and churches who needed the most help or, at the very least, a shot of encouragement, were the same locations these destructive teams had focused on.

What these mission leaders had not considered was that many of these smaller communities and churches cannot support a pastor and family. Many of these faithful leaders work other jobs to support their callings, and some even work to help pay the church light bill. The pastor who mentioned "putting out fires" was talking about the relational mess he was left with. Young men from the incoming youth mission team were much more focused on reaching the local girls in the area than serving his church or community.

"And why was their missions leader so lax that his teens could be found paired off in various parts of my church, doing God knows what?!"

What do you say to that? I answered, "Good question, Pastor!"

I knew that these were the churches, communities and pastors that God was calling me to encourage. I was given a vision to train up passionate teams of youth to come alongside these leaders and help them catapult their local vision. To have this influence, I would need to raise the bar. After weeks of speaking to pastors and hearing the same story repeated over and over, I knew I needed to lay out a plan.

My first objective was to persuade just one pastor to open his door to my team. Then I would build off of that encounter. Having been raised in a minister's home my whole life, I had a good idea of what they actually needed, as well as those things they would not like repeated. I knew the mission needed to be a win for both parties, not one-sided. We needed to bring legitimate hearts to serve, and that service must leave a positive residual effect on the church body and pastor. Likewise, there needed to be opportunities for youth to experience serving that body and that community.

Bringing some testimonies and sermons would not be enough to create a lasting blessing. So I made a list of non-negotiable points:

- We would be completely self-sufficient, be a blessing and not a burden.
- We would bring our own paper products, plates, cups, bowls, paper towels, toilet paper, etc. We would bring more than we would need, so we could leave them stocked up.
- We would bring enough cleaning products for our stay, as well as plenty to leave behind.
- We would bring all of our food and prepare all of our meals. Our food inventory would include feeding the pastor and his family each day and leave plenty for their (usually empty) pantry.
- We would bring a check or cash to offset the

utilities for a large group visiting and using their facility.

- We would buy a new vacuum cleaner, use it while we were there and leave it with them. (Our lead trip team would identify such needs.)
- We would even pre-purchase a sound system, if needed.

My intent was to overwhelm them with blessing and encouragement in the name of mission work. After our team's departure, I wanted them to actually miss us, to have wonderful memories, knowing that someone cared and that someone did them right. I wanted them to feel like someone bent over backward to bless their family, ministry, community and facilities.

During the lead trip, we would find out their needs, desires and vision and then go home and form the ministry agenda around those findings. Many times, leaders of missions will get a word, a passion and often a method locked into their heart. But it ends up not being the thing that the local pastor/leader wanted or needed.

As we trained our team and imparted the vision, we would also lay out a ministry assignment for each person. From luggage detail, sound equipment techs, building and repair team, drivers, cooks, street ministry organizers, promotional team, hospitality team, etc., I think you get the point. We would also make it clear to our team that my wife and I would focus on encouraging the pastor and his family. They knew that this would be our foundational purpose for the trip. My father would always tell me when I was a young minister, "If you don't do anything else, son, be a blessing to that pastor."

My convincing finally worked with one dear pastor serving a little church way off the grid, in the foothills of Northern California. He'd had a negative experience, similar to those previously described, and had closed the door to other teams, until now. Something stirred in his heart as we met, and he was ready to take a chance with me.

I recall sitting down with him the day before we left, and tears were running down his face as he tried to thank me for each and every thing our team had done. "This church has never looked so clean before!" He and his wife were overwhelmed with thanksgiving. He was one of those who worked an outside job to keep things running at the church, and instead of a financial burden being left on his shoulders, we left him with a blessing. New visitors came to the church, attendance grew and, most importantly, people came to know Jesus. Supporting the local vision will maximize the efforts of your team and your mission.

Finding Refuge

We had been traveling the river system for more than 20 hours and needed to find a place to camp. The upcoming island had high banks and looked promising. We hit the landing a little harder than planned and dumped a pile of dirt on the bow. Jeremiah, one of the young men on my team, attempted a hasty jump up to the extended shore, only to feel the ground break through under his feet. He was quickly taken underwater by the swift current of the Yukon.

I stepped to the front of the boat to find one hand clenching tight to the rim of the boat. After an exhaustive struggle to pull him out of the river, we both ventured out of the boat and onto the island to survey its camping potential.

Finding the right location to camp overnight with a large team is a safety issue. There are several factors to consider. Is it on high ground? If too low, the water level can rise and flood your camp. Is it level enough? If too much incline, sleeping will be challenging. Is the area large enough for a big team? What's the wind direction? Is it a safe place for a fire? Is it too close to the brush or woods area? Too close and the bugs will be thick, and the bears will have easy access. Is the foundation firm? Does the sand sit on rock, or does it consist of only sand? We would find the answer to this last question much sooner than desired.

As we walked from the boat to a large clearing, the ground broke through, and we were up to our chests in quicksand. Yes, I know, this sounds like some crazy Amazon jungle story or something that would happen in a faraway desert. Who would have thought, quicksand on the Yukon River?!

Jeremiah shifted into panic mode and began to use my body as his escape ladder. I was thinking, as I sank deeper under my weight and his, *Oh, this is just great. I just saved his life, and now he's gonna secure my death in this pit!*

While "Cowboy Dan," one of my staff, was running back to the boat to get a rope, I was clenching my shotgun in my left hand and fighting off Jeremiah with my right. I must confess, I did consider shooting him in the leg. Hey, sometimes on a mission trip, you operate in the flesh! Escaping the furious river current and the sandpit of death, we decided that this island was not suitable to make camp. Relational conflict is bound to happen. But most of these conflicts can be avoided through creating environments for the team to develop unity prior to the mission.

Being diligent to preserve the unity of the Spirit in the bond of peace (Ephesians 4:3).

Mission Team Ministry Training

There IS a proper way to establish ministry influence and increase your potential for greater success. Giving your team opportunities to grow before they go will build self-confidence, as well as unity in the team. Never assume everyone is on the same page of ministry belief. People will have a tendency to minister to others the way that they were ministered to. Although their approach may be well accepted in their home church, that same approach may be offensive to another culture.

I recall a well-meaning minister who felt it was his calling to make sure every person he prayed for hit the ground. If they didn't make this move by the leading of the Holy Spirit, he would gladly help them get down there. The power of God slammed him to the ground when he first came to the Lord, and he was sure the rest of the planet needed that same experience.

Develop a training schedule with intent. Make each time of learning and impartation a building block to the next time of teaching. The areas of training will differ, depending on the culture and people you are preparing for. Here are a few basic categories you may need to cover:

Prayer and Fasting

Scheduling times of unified prayer is especially crucial in building unity and building up the collective empowerment needed to find success in the field.

Schedule times of fasting as a team. It's during these times of fasting that we are most sensitive to the voice of the Lord.

Local Protocol

The intel from your lead trip will guide you in the lifestyle protocol to train for. Remember, same Gospel, but often different methods are needed. (More on this in the next chapter.)

Gifts of the Spirit

Study and teach 1 Corinthians 12, and encourage the team to utilize the nine spiritual gifts:

1. Words of wisdom
2. Words of knowledge
3. Faith
4. Gifts of healing
5. Working of miracles
6. Prophecy
7. Discerning of spirits
8. Kinds of tongues
9. Interpretation of tongues

Yes, these are for us today! Use them.

Same-Gender Ministry

Train men to minister to men and women to minister to women. This will help avoid misunderstandings, as well as inappropriate touch. Use wisdom when ministering the laying on of hands. You may not know what abuse the person you are praying for has experienced.

Personal Boundaries

Train your team to respect the personal boundaries of others. Learn the culture, and keep in mind that those who you are reaching may have had negative experience with touch and/or close proximity. Focus on building trust with people, which will go a long way in the field.

Ministry Assignments

Use your team in its strengths, and encourage all to walk in their God-given gifts. If hospitality is their strength, don't push them to preach. Use these scheduled times to find the areas where each team member thrives, and help them maximize their efforts.

Using Your Authority

Teach the team to recognize the power they have at their disposal.

³⁵But Jesus rebuked him, saying, "Be quiet and come out of him!" And when the demon had thrown him down in the midst of the people, he came out of him without doing him any harm. ³⁶And amazement came upon them all, and they began talking with one another saying, "What is this message? For with authority and power He commands the unclean spirits and they come out." ³⁷And the report about Him was spreading into every locality in the surrounding district (Luke 4:35-37).

The "authority and power" that they recognized then is the same "authority and power" passed on to us today.

Group Communion

I have yet to find a better way to "build and sustain unity" in a team than joining together in communion. This practice of confession and embracing the new blood covenant clears the air and keeps offense from infecting and undermining the unity of the team.

The Meal That Heals by Perry Stone reminds us of what a powerful healing tool communion can be in our lives. Jentezen Franklin writes in the foreword: "Partaking of Communion gives life to your marriage, your church and your physical body. It really is the meal that heals."

That "life" must be taken into the mission field and imparted to the rejected, the hurting, the wounded and the lost! They don't simply need information. They need impartation. Information is helpful, but impartation is transforming.

Communion directs our attention back to God's covenant of healing, which we must take into our mission field. One of the most wonderful byproducts of team communion is an increase in the Holy Spirit's power on individuals. And this combined anointing will empower your mission to be accomplished.

God also testified with them, both by signs and wonders and by various miracles and by gifts of the Holy Spirit according to His own will (Hebrews 2:4).

A united purpose won't simply happen because we have a vision to reach the lost. The level of unity we need to succeed in the mission field comes with focused planning. As we invest our time, resources and passion into building up unity in every aspect of our mission preparation, we then will enjoy the fruit of our labor. A united purpose!

Chapter Eight
Secret Weapon

A gift opens the way for the giver and ushers him into the presence of the great. (Proverbs 18:16, NIV)

Finding the Missing Link

I had no idea just how powerful this mission trip would be. This was my first Alaskan village mission endeavor, a very special mission that would lead to countless more. This powerful key, called "protocol," would unlock the hearts and the community at levels I could not have imagined.

In the early stages of planning this outreach, the Lord spoke very clearly to me in my heart. It happened in my office. *You don't know what you are doing.* I quickly started rebuking this voice, knowing that it must be the enemy. I rebuked and rebuked, but I kept hearing this voice. It then followed with, *All of your missions experience won't help you. This is a different culture and a different people. Find help.*

The words may have seemed harsh, but the voice was not condemning in any way. As I began to humbly embrace these words, I could feel the peace and presence of God. I began to weep and open my heart to the next step that God was leading me to take.

Somehow, I knew what to do. I began to call around looking for a Native minister who could tutor me in the culture of the indigenous people in this region. There seemed to be a core theme in what I was learning from him, one word that kept coming to the surface in all he spoke: "protocol."

I was moved by an urgency and started walking through the local protocol of that village shortly after landing in Shaktoolik. "Where can I find the mayor?" I asked the local pastor. I was told he could be found on the south side of the village, working on the generators that power the village. I was also told that I would be wasting my time, as he had never set foot in the church and would not receive my invitation with any openness. He was not fond of outsiders, and I certainly fit that profile.

When I found him, he was much shorter than I expected, an elderly man in his 70s, rugged-looking and bent over from a curved back. My introduction was returned by a stern glare, a look that appeared to be saying, "Why are you on my land?"

The words that I spoke next would completely remove the awkward tension in the air. "I want to thank you for allowing me and my team to visit your land. I have purchased a very special gift for you, and I would like to honor you with it in front of your people. It would be a great honor if you came tonight at 7 o'clock for this important gathering." His countenance transformed within moments, he shook my hand and said he would be there. The local pastor was very surprised and pleased, to say the least.

I knew this honoring service would be a special event, but I had no idea just how powerful it would be. I didn't speak long, but with great sincerity. I honored his title and position. I spoke to his strength as a man. I blessed his difficult task of leading his people and spoke of the strength and power of his history, his great works and his potential. I then uncovered a wonderful and expensive work of Native Art and presented it to him. You could hear the "oohs" and "aahs" from the audience. I would find out later that no one had ever honored this leader publicly. The smile that formed on his face revealed a heart that was overwhelmed with joy and evident signs of inner healing. Tears began to run down his face, but he didn't wipe a single tear, as if he didn't want to bring attention to his emotions. He then gathered himself together, put on a slightly more serious look and spoke some words that would change the spiritual environment of the entire village. "You are welcome on our land. I give you the key to my village. You can do anything you want and minister to our people." He then put out his hand of approval.

I was not prepared for what took place next. As we exited the service and walked through the village, everyone we encountered was not only open to ministry, but actually expected it.

As we approached people, they would throw down their cigarettes and put out their hands for prayer. As we approached one man, a man who was not at the protocol event, he looked up at us, threw down his alcohol, lifted his hands and bowed his head for prayer. We were amazed at the openness of the people.

Word travels fast in a small village, and the word had gotten out to every corner of this community about how we had honored their leader and that the mayor had given us the keys to his village. What it meant to the people was that if he gave his stamp of approval, then they must, also. Protocol, I came to realize, is the missing link to successful missions.

Protocol? What Is It?

Not much has been written on the subject of protocol. Protocol appears to be a seemingly insignificant word to most, not a word heard often among mission leaders and rarely from a pulpit. I must admit, prior to the late 1990s, this word had virtually no personal meaning for me. It took a process to change my thinking.

Secret Weapon

I hope to take you on a journey as you walk through the pages of this chapter. This is a journey that the Lord put me on in 1998, a journey that continued to increase my hunger to fully understand protocol and how it relates to the life of ministry.

To me, protocol appeared to be something that a national government leader might be interested in, but never a regular guy like me. From the view of a minister, I certainly could not see this thing called protocol used in a spiritual application. It appeared to be another manmade hoop to jump through, only contributing to the slowing down of my ministry goals and agenda. I later came to understand that nothing could have been further from the truth. Rather than slow the mission down, protocol put things in hyper-drive.

When I began to step into the realm of practicing protocol, I immediately started experiencing a new level of success in my ministry ventures. It was as if I had stumbled onto some top-secret weapon for ministering to other cultures and people groups.

As I researched the Word of God, I found that this "top-secret weapon" was actually an obvious method of operation, exemplified throughout scriptures. I simply had bypassed its purpose, meaning and application over the years.

During my second mission trip into an Athabascan Native village, a Native evangelist pulled me aside and said these words, "You must be doing something right. I've been coming to this village for seven years, and they can't even remember my name. Yet they have accepted you with open arms!" As he spoke these words, I knew that the opening of hearts came from the supernatural work of the Holy Spirit. It sure wasn't due to our "coolness" or talents. It was the display of protocol that had released God's favor all over our mission.

As we dig into this "secret weapon" called protocol, let's start with the basic meaning of the word.

pro·to·col
the customs and regulations dealing with
diplomatic formality, precedence and etiquette
(Dictionary.com)

Webster's definition:
The ceremonial forms and courtesies that are
established as proper and correct

Allow me to simplify. Protocol is the approaching, greeting, speaking, gifting and honoring within the cultural ceremonial forms, customs and courtesies established by a given people group. Let's take a closer look at these five areas.

1) Approaching

How we enter a community, city, village or tribe affects just how successful our mission effort will be, as well as how long we are welcome. Too often, a missionary, pastor or outreach team must exit a community early, due to the chain reaction of improper entry. (More on this later.)

How we enter a home, office or local facility will also be an indicator to others of what our attitude and motives might be. Our physical and verbal approach will make either a positive or negative impression.

2) Greeting

Proper methods of greeting are crucial to finding necessary favor for effective ministry. Knowing who to greet, how to greet, when to greet and where to greet will keep doors swinging wide open, one after another. Learning the correct greeting sequence of a culture can make a major difference in being accepted.

Much of the honoring that takes place is somewhat "incognito." Alaskan example: If I were to enter a village tribal hall and walk past an elder to greet a teen I know, that elder would feel dishonored, although he would never tell me. If, however, upon entering the building I first looked to see who was there, I would recognize the elder, approach him from his front and, if he is sitting, I would go to one knee before I speak to him. He would feel honored by me, and others would see this display of honor that is fitting to their protocol.

3) Speaking

We Westerners are known for our abundance in speech. We certainly enjoy talking. In much of our culture, we find ourselves comfortable with talking over one another. We will even raise our voice to be heard over another person. But when we speak to a people group using *their* methods of speaking, we increase our chances of being heard.

Many cultures look at us as people who talk too much, and in most cases, I would have to say I agree with them. I recall a time when an elder in a village was telling us stories, and he turned to one young man and said, "You must be a wise man because you keep quiet and listen." Later, this young man gave me a look, indicating he and I both knew that he had just received a label that the entire team wished was true. He was most definitely challenged in that area; happily, he was caught with his mouth closed at the right time.

Even a fool, when he keeps silent, is considered wise; when he closes his lips, he is considered prudent (Proverbs 17:28).

Sometimes, less is more.

The volume that we use can make a difference as well. In some cultures, a loud and aggressive voice may show strength, while in others, the soft-spoken word shows a greater strength and respect. Among the Athabascan Indians of Alaska, speaking in a soft tone will draw the listener in closer, to better hear. This is a way to honor them in speech.

4) Gifting

"Better to give than to receive," a verse we have all heard, but just maybe not completely made central in our lives. Our Western church culture will give, but usually out of our excess.

In Genesis 32, Jacob sent many worthy gifts ahead of him. Thousands of rams and goats as well as silver were brought to Hezekiah, king of Judah, in 2 Chronicles 17, lavishing him with gifts of honor.

In 2 Chronicles 32:23, many brought offerings to Jerusalem for the Lord, as well as valuable gifts for Hezekiah. From then on, he was highly regarded by all the nations.

Note that people brought "valuable gifts" to the king. They didn't stop by Desert-Mart on their way to the king's palace and grab some camel-print sandals on discount. They planned ahead. They did their homework, researched what a king would be pleased with and prepared their gifts accordingly.

The gift must cost us something.

In 2 Samuel 24, King David desired to buy some land from Araunah so he could build an altar to make a sacrifice unto the Lord. David makes the offer to purchase it, but Araunah offers the land to King David for free.

23 "Everything, O king, Araunah gives to the king." And Araunah said to the king, "May the Lord your God accept you." 24 However, the king said to Araunah, "No, but I will surely buy it from you for a price, for I will not offer burnt offerings to the Lord my God which cost me nothing." So David bought the threshing floor and the oxen for fifty shekels of silver. 25 David built there an altar to the Lord and offered burnt offerings and peace offerings. Thus the

Lord was moved by prayer for the land, and the plague was held back from Israel (2 Samuel 24:23-25).

David insisted on paying for the threshing floor because he would not sacrifice to the Lord offerings that cost him nothing. He also understood the ways of the Lord, knowing that if he truly wanted to move the hand of God, his sacrificial ceremony must be sincere, and the gifts offered up must be of great worth. This altar and sacrifice were serious things, as he would be asking God to hold back plague from the land. Isn't that what we, as missionaries, want? To see God remove spiritual plague from the land? Gifting breathes life into the act of honoring.

5) Honoring

Honoring? Should we honor unbelievers? What is honoring? There are so many different views on this, it can get your brain in a swirl. Often, we find it so confusing or overwhelming we simply don't make it a part of our mission planning. But the power of honoring is grossly underestimated.

You will find honoring and gifting are intertwined with most aspects of protocol in any culture. When we honor people, we greatly increase our opportunities to earn a voice through that honoring.

*The Lord says, "These people come near to Me with their mouth and **honor** Me with their lips, but their hearts are far from Me. Their worship of Me is made up only of rules taught by men" (Isaiah 29:13).*

Secret Weapon

True honoring must be seen in our actions and our investment, not just our words.

The scripture gives many examples of honoring posture, such as in Genesis 43, where Joseph's brothers brought gifts that they had prepared and bowed low to pay him honor.

On the third day a man arrived from Saul's camp, with his clothes torn and with dust on his head. When he came to David, he fell to the ground to pay him honor (2 Samuel 1:2).

Just as important as the physical posture is the posture of our heart. This inner posturing will show up in the way we live, not just at an event or ceremony. When honor is in our hearts, it will be manifest in every area of our lives.

Honor your father and your mother, as the LORD your God has commanded you, so that you may live long and that it may go well with you in the land the LORD your God is giving you (Deuteronomy 5:16).

You know the commandments: 'Do not commit adultery, do not murder, do not steal, do not give false testimony, honor your father and mother' (Luke 18:20).

Teaching a team to honor in the mission field is much easier than teaching them to honor their family when they get home. If our honoring stays in the field, it has not yet found its way into the heart of the mission or the hearts of the missionary.

In 2 Samuel 23, we see that Benaiah, one of David's mighty men, did great exploits for the king. He killed two of Moab's greatest men, he killed a lion in a pit, he came against a huge Egyptian with a club, he took the spear from this monster of a man and killed him with it.

He was held in greater honor than any of the Thirty, but he was not included among the Three. <u>And David put him in charge of his bodyguard.</u>

When we honor the way God has shown us to honor, we will be promoted! Wow, the very thing many are striving for can be obtained by serving and honoring others.

Some of us are old enough to have observed the removal of honor that took place in America during the '60s, '70s and '80s. From the political realm to the church, and even in the home, we can see the decay of honor that has taken place. Now, looking back, we can pinpoint the schemes of the enemy to remove a heart of honor from our culture:

- Those with title fell.
- The national respect was lost.
- Compromise and justifications were made.

There will always be mistakes and failures made by men and women in leadership, because they are simply men and women, just like you and me. So there was never a justifiable reason to walk away from the teaching of Christ, simply because a spiritual leader fell. Excuses were made, but not reasons.

When we justify our wrong reactions to someone's wrong actions, we have simply revealed the rebellion that taints our heart. That inner rebellion will fight all honorable thinking. Wrong reactions to wrong actions are justifiable to the rebellious heart.

This inner dishonor will influence actions and reaction in our daily life. One can recognize it through our interaction with authority. Have you ever had an issue with honoring a leader in your life? Just imagine one of King David's "Mighty Men" approaching him and saying, "What's up, Dave?" They knew him well. They knew him personally. Some had been with him from the beginning and grew up with him. Yet, they honored the position God had assigned to David, and that position was called "King."

Furthermore, we don't have the luxury of only honoring those we like. King David benefited from the law of "sowing and reaping" as he was honored by his men because they watched him honor King Saul, who was going far out of his way to murder David. Maybe you have a personality conflict with your pastor, or find your boss to be overbearing and obnoxious, or just maybe you don't care much for the president. When we honor those in authority, we are honoring a position that God created, and our personal opinion has no dominion.

When the woman from Tekoa went to the king, she fell with her face to the ground to pay him honor, and she said, "Help me, O king!" (2 Samuel 14:4).

I found the phrase "O king" 39 times in the pages of the Bible, spoken by people who were approaching and communicating with the king of their day. After spending the night in the lions' den, at the decree of the king, Daniel proclaimed, "**O king**, live forever!" We have a warped view in our church culture if we only want to honor those we like, those who like us or maybe those who agree with our ideas.

Be devoted to one another in brotherly love; give preference to one another in honor (Romans 12:10).

The NIV reads, *Be devoted to one another in brotherly love. Honor one another above yourselves.* I believe that "selective honoring" comes from a spirit of selfishness. This self-focused view of life keeps us from understanding or desiring the life of honor.

Honor all people, love the brotherhood, fear God, honor the king (1 Peter 2:17).

Did you happen to notice that this directive to "honor the king" did not come with an "opinion clause"? If we withhold honor because we deem the person unworthy, then we have given our opinion equal authority to the Word of the Lord.

The elders who rule well are to be considered worthy of double honor, especially those who work hard at preaching and teaching (1 Timothy 5:17).

Dishonoring does not need a plan. It comes automatically when we don't make plans to honor.

"If you do not listen, and if you do not take it to heart to give honor to My name," says the LORD of hosts, "then I will send the curse upon you and I will curse your blessings; and indeed, I have cursed them already, because you are not taking it to heart" (Malachi 2:2).

Secret Weapon

True honoring comes from the heart and will always be seen in our actions. How can we honor the Lord? One effective way is by honoring those that He has put over us. As we honor them, we are actually honoring God. Honoring will bust open doors that you and I could never get through on our own.

৯৯৯

Now that we have covered the foundations of what protocol is, it's time to back up the truck and talk about the process of getting to the mission field in the first place.

Let me start by saying that I do understand that there are ministry outreaches where we are unable to seek proper protocol. Mission fields that if we were to make ourselves known, it would be a detriment to the mission and most likely risk harm and imprisonment. Mission endeavors that require us to disobey the laws of the land (such as smuggling Bibles) to obey the written and spoken mandate of God. However, these stealth-like mission maneuvers make up the smaller percentage of mission work.

If you have any experience in missions or local church ministry, then I'm sure you have a story or two of a missionary work or church that simply never grows. On the contrary, that ministry seems to always have inner conflict and an overall history of failure. "Maybe they need a new pastor?" some might say. Yet, over the years, nearly every person holding any position there was a suspect at one time or another. Could the issue be found in its foundations?

Leadership might come and go and heartfelt attempts made to turn the sinking ship around, but nothing seems to help, nothing ever works. Some would even venture to say, "Maybe that place is cursed?" And maybe they are not that far off.

Okay, I know that I got some theologians stirred up about now, ready to give me a lecture. But before you heat up the tar and find a bag of feathers, stay with me here. I do agree with you that there is power in the name of Jesus and that the Son of God can use His resurrection power to move mountains. He told His disciples that with the faith of a mustard seed they could speak to a mountain and tell it where to go. Or, more accurately, send it to the sea.

However, there is an honoring of authority that Jesus Himself practiced. Seeking permission from the proper spiritual or governing authorities was a practice of Christ, as well as His followers. Even Moses used the protocol of that kingdom when he approached the heathen ruler Pharaoh.

I propose to you that many of these struggling locations, on the mission field or the church in your city, were not built on property that was acquired using the protocol of that day. Although the teaching of honor and protocol has been prevalent over the years, I would guess it has not always been a teaching imparted in our schools of higher learning, including our many faith-based institutions.

A passion for the mission and a dogmatic posture sent many missionaries into the field saying, "By God, I'm gonna preach to these people if it's the last thing I do!" And, for some, it was. For many others, they caved to the pressures of never being accepted and moved to let someone else fill that same non-accepted role. As they escaped the very field they were called to, answers were fleeting, reasons were fabricated, blame was placed and confusion began to kill their faith. They had done everything textbook; they fasted and prayed like never before. But the breakthrough they were expecting never broke through.

This is where even the most fundamental steps of spiritual mapping can be helpful in providing insight, information, revelation and confirmed direction before proceeding with a plan. While I'm not one to jump in and ride the current wave of belief or methodology, I have personally gained much helpful insight, information, revelation and confirmed direction from even the most fundamental steps of spiritual mapping.

Attempting to copycat the successes of our past is one of the greatest mistakes we make in ministry. Just because it worked amazingly in the past does not guarantee it will work the same way today. Before we set foot in the mission field to administer our plan, we should do some homework and gather insightful knowledge that could greatly affect our methods and success. "Our level of success on the mission field is directly related to the way we entered." If this statement has any truth to it, then implementing some basic elements of spiritual mapping is to our advantage.

If there is a chapter in this book that inspired the title *Mission Accomplished*, it is certainly this one. I can think of no other subject that affects our success more than the practice of protocol and honoring. And, if dishonoring of the very people we want to reach is in the history of the land, we need to understand the process to bring healing from that illegal entry.

Let's take a moment and break down these words of Jesus.

I tell you the truth, the man who does not enter the sheep pen by the gate, but climbs in by some other way, is a thief and a robber (John 10:1).

The method matters. There is a door we should enter, and that door is designed by that unique culture. The man who enters by the gate is the shepherd of his sheep. When you have nothing to hide, you walk in through the main gate. The proper way gives favor.

The watchman opens the gate for him, and the sheep listen to his voice. He calls his own sheep by name and leads them out. The watchman opened the door because he can recognize a true shepherd when he sees one. By honoring the watchman, positive results are the reward.

When the shepherd has brought out all his own, he goes on ahead of them, and his sheep follow him because they know his voice. Proper protocol breeds loyalty. When proper protocol has been established, the sheep will also recognize a real shepherd and follow him as he follows

Christ. But they will never follow a stranger; in fact, they will run away from him because they do not recognize a stranger's voice. A great leader can be viewed by the sheep as a thief, rather than a true shepherd, when he bypasses the gatekeeper. Gatekeepers keep a record of who goes out and who comes in. This is often what we in the church experience on the mission field.

Wrong entry, no favor. No favor, bad soil. Bad soil, no planting. No planting, no harvest.

It's not that missionaries or pastors were not wanted in their village. It's that permission was never asked. They gained access by way of acquiring land from someone desperate to sell, and the missionary never spoke with the chief, never asked permission of the village council. Two generations later, that offense still resonates in the hearts of the community. God designed the protocol of honoring the gatekeepers, and it works.

Correcting a Wrong

There might be times in ministry that we need to take a step back before we can move forward. Researching the original type of entry that was made may be required. The way that building or property was acquired, as well as the way that established ministry was conceived, makes a difference today.

If I were to move onto your property without ever asking your permission, I would be hard pressed to find any favor from you or your family. And if 30 years later, others came to build on my work (on your land), I would imagine they would find the same resistance from your offspring.

Administering repentance to the people for the hurts brought on by former leaders is a Biblical precedence that forms the foundation for cultivating healing and restoration. Often this restoring is needed before we can move ahead with our mission.

I have seen this offer of repentance beautifully plant seeds of healing. Healed hearts condition the people to invite the once uninvited into their community.

The Power of Gifting

We had boated into the village early in the morning, after a night's stay on an island for rest. The pastor whose property we were scheduled to stay on was out of the area, and the church was two miles from the river. I made an executive decision to stay near the riverbank for the next few days, as that is where the locals were gathering as they prepared their fish wheels and nets for the king salmon season.

You go where the people are. They are who we came to minister to, and if they are here, staying somewhere farther away from them would not be wisdom at work. Besides, the thought of moving all the gear and supplies back and forth did not appeal to me.

Now the question was, "Where do we make camp?" There was a large grassy area just up from the riverbank, an area used over the years for official Native gatherings.

But I would need permission; you don't just make camp on Native land without proper permission. I asked a local if he knew where I could find the chief of the village, and he pointed to a field next to the very spot I had my eyes on.

The chief was working in a community garden, and as I approached behind him, I purposely made some noise so I wouldn't startle him. "Excuse me, are you the chief?"

He actually glared at me, sized me up and said, "I'm the chief. Who wants to know?"

When gifting a leader, I would always recommend doing so in a public community setting for several reasons:

1. The honor has greater impact on the receiver when a public group witnesses him being honored.
2. Those watching will be encouraged and blessed to see one of their leaders respected publicly.
3. The larger the group, the greater the opportunity to bring emotional healing to both the honored one and those watching.

This was one of those situations where I didn't have the luxury of waiting on a protocol event. Not knowing just how this might go down, I had a new Buck knife ready in my back pocket, one I had purchased for him months prior.

I responded to his stern question by telling him what a

privilege it was to meet him and how I had purchased him a special gift, in hopes of a chance to honor him with it. I reached behind and grabbed the large yellow box that had the bold Buck logo plastered all over it.

He opened the box quickly, and in his haste the knife fell to the ground. The look of embarrassment left his face quickly as he recovered the shiny new hunting knife. The smile on his face grew as he pulled the Buck from its leather sheath. I could tell he was impressed by the quality.

He then turned around and started waving the gift in the air. He was yelling across the field to some friends who were with him. "He gave me a knife! It's a real nice one! He gave me a knife!" After getting the attention of his buddies, he turned back around to me, gathered his thoughts and emotions and spoke these words: "You can do whatever you need to do in my village. You can stay on our land as long as you wish. If any man gives you a problem, you come to me, and I will take care of him."

He smiled real big, thanked me and started walking away. But then he quickly turned around, as if he had forgotten something, and said, "If any woman gives you trouble, I'll take care of her, too!" He let out a laugh and walked over to his friends to show off his new possession.

Needless to say, we made one massive tent city on the very location I had my eye on. Moreover, the nearest homeowner, inspired by one happy and aggressive chief, was glad to give us power for our sound equipment. An effective ministry was then enjoyed by our team.

I simply will not travel to any community without a

stash of protocol gifts. In most cases, I will have researched the leaders (pastors, mayors, chiefs, elders, etc.) far in advance and will have selected a gift that fits their need and/or personality. No matter how well I plan, however, there are always those unplanned guests, leaders or officials that I want to honor with a protocol gift at a moment's notice. So I pack accordingly.

Ready In Season and Out of Season

You can prepare for unplanned opportunities by making gifts a part of your outreach or missions budget. Let me explain. Every ministry team I take into the field will have a "protocol gift" fee added to their total missions trip cost. It might be as little as $25. But, depending on the size of the team, that gives me a nice foundation of funds to work with.

I also gather nice gifts throughout the year to use for such times. I actually have a large ActionPacker bin made by Rubbermaid that I call "my gift box," and I keep it supplied with quality items with which to bless others. My habit is not to just hand these gifts out. I inquire of the Lord, "Who was this gift intended for?" And without fail, it's always just the very thing that would bless the right person.

For planned honoring opportunities, do some research and learn what might be an appropriate gift for that person in his or her culture.

A gift opens the way for the giver and ushers him into the presence of the great (Proverbs 18:16, NIV).

A man's gift makes room for him, and brings him before great men (Proverbs 18:16, NASB).

There are three important things that will take place as a direct result of this giving process:

1) The gift opens the way to the giver.

There are doors designed for the people of God to walk through. And yet many, if not most, ministers of the Gospel of Jesus Christ will never venture through these thresholds. Not because they lack desire, but simply because they did not practice the foundational protocol called "gifting." Yes, your spiritual gift can open doors. But often it takes a physical gift to open a heart that will embrace the spiritual.

2) The gift ushers the giver into opportunity.

We use the word "opportunity" lightly, as if opportunity is automatic. Without opportunity, we will never see the "inside" or "inner circle" of the location we are called to serve.

op·por·tu·ni·ty
1. an appropriate or favorable time or occasion
2. a situation or condition favorable for attainment of a goal
3. a good position, chance or prospect, as for advancement or success

You see that, in this definition, opportunity is not

simply getting a chance, and not everyone is entitled to it. In sports, every time you win a game, you have earned the opportunity to move on to the next game. Each level successfully conquered moves you closer to the goal. And not every team gets that opportunity.

3) The action places the giver in the presence of influential people.

God's favor will always be transferred through people of influence. Without people of influence involved in our ministry, we will struggle to accomplish the dreams that God put in our hearts. The accomplishment of our dreams will be a byproduct of protocol gifting.

For far too long, protocol has been the missing link in successful missions. Join me in restoring a Biblical method of honor that will help secure the priceless fruit of our mission labor.

Restoring Honor

Our protocol ceremony of honoring the village elders was well received, and many tears of appreciation were shown, especially as I publicly gifted the oldest woman in the village. This dear elder, who was proud to have raised a whaling captain, was now shedding tears as she responded to this honor, saying, "I can't remember being honored in front of people like this before." I was completely taken back!

Wow, this amazing jewel in her 90s had not been

honored? Did I get their protocol wrong? As we closed the service, a man in his 60s waved for me to come to the back of the room. As I walked toward him, his eyes appeared to be intense, as if he was not very happy with the service. Sure that I was about to get a verbal spanking, I was rewinding each of the night's events through my head. *I must have offended them,* I thought. But before I could formulate a good apology, I was standing in front of him.

A tear was running down the weathered cheek of this Yupik Siberian Eskimo elder as he began to speak. "Thank you for reminding me of our protocol. Our people once honored each other. I haven't seen this in a long time. Thank you."

God is so amazing. He can use some white guy to remind an indigenous people of the honor they once valued. What a great privilege to restore the ancient protocol of a culture, a protocol once immersed in honor, an honor that comes from the very heart of God. Anointed success in the field is the byproduct of honoring protocol.

Back to Shaktoolik

As a direct result of practicing protocol and honoring the mayor in this Eskimo village, a culture of honor was put into effect. We experienced fruit that only the Holy Spirit could produce. The first night, after the service, we gathered large piles of driftwood and had a massive fire on the beach. We knew it would draw young people, especially those many teens who would not show up inside the church walls. Just as intended, the fire drew the young people each night. It was a great environment to connect with them and pray for them.

But what we had not intended to take place would amaze us each night. Locals of all ages started bringing boxes, bags and sacks full of items to burn. Porn magazines, movies, music, drugs, alcohol and drug paraphernalia. Every night. You could see the black cloud of smoke for miles!

This move was supernatural. We never promoted a cleansing fire or persuaded them to come. They were simply convicted of the Holy Spirit and brought these things to the fire on their own. After throwing items in the flames, they would stay around the fire to be prayed for. There was no need to hunt down ministry opportunities. They willingly came to us. With loaded arms and open hearts, they came ready to meet Jesus. Honoring God's way will bring needed healing and open the hearts of people, the very people you are mandated to reach on your next mission.

CHAPTER NINE

RELATIONAL KEYS

And He took them in His arms and began blessing them,
laying His hands on them. (Mark 10:16)

The King of Kings

After three weeks of running their fish wheel nearly 24/7, they had only caught two king salmon. For these indigenous families, that was a real concern. Catching enough salmon to get their families through the next winter was not a nicety. It was a necessity.

"Can we pray over your fish wheel?" I asked, as we came ashore with our boats. We must have looked like the Clampetts from *The Beverly Hillbillies* show with our overloaded boats. Reluctant at first, they agreed to let us pray. After praying over their fish wheel, we made conversation, then headed downriver. The next village was about 25 miles away.

The very next day, we encountered some of their fish camp family walking up from the riverbank. "Hey, Pastor! Your prayers worked!" said a young boy, who was overwhelmed by the 50-pound salmon in his arms. This fish was as tall as he was. Then he and his family approached me and gave us a large king salmon. "We caught nine kings!" he kept saying. He continued to thank us for the prayers and repeat the story to those around him, "We only got two kings in weeks, and after the prayer, we caught nine!"

This king salmon was a real blessing to our team and was more than enough for dinner that evening. Others came around and listened to the stories of our "fish wheel prayer," and we could see walls being lowered simply because of the blessing of fish. Fish speaks to their actual needs and to their culture.

We could also see God using this blessing to open up doors to relationships that remain strong to this day. You see, the deeper the connection with people, the wider other doors will fly open for ministry.

Taking advantage of what God has done through your ministry is a valuable step in building relationships. When God blesses, heals or shows Himself through answered prayer, I believe God always has multiple reasons. I believe that one of the purposes is to open doors to the hearts of people groups. Hearts were wide open that day and to bypass this opportunity would be a great God opportunity missed. Your greatest effectiveness in missions will involve your greatest relationship investments.

Police in the Park

This street outreach, called the "F40," was a mission that was equally feared and anticipated by those students scheduled to go. F40 was simply fasting for 40 hours while living on the streets and loving the homeless. No sleeping bag, no suitcase, no camping gear and no guarantee of a restroom. Those on this training mission could only have a small section of a tarp, one small daypack, a water bottle and a Bible in their ministry arsenal. They could take cash, but only to buy food for those living on the street. The team would be fasting.

The vision that the Lord gave me for the F40 came out of this truth: "You can't really minister to the homeless while traveling in an air-conditioned church van with a full stomach." The Holy Spirit impressed on my heart that our students would receive fresh revelation as they ministered to people on the street if they were in the same condition.

Wow, did it ever work! More personal revelation and breaking down of barriers to spiritual growth took place through this 40-hour event than on any other mission.

Too often, our ministry plans aren't effective simply because we bypassed the relational part of protocol. Knowing that I would be bringing a large team of young adults into the core of the city to "live homeless" for two days, I decided to first inform the chief of police. I came prepared. I had done my homework, and I knew that it was not against any city ordinance to do so. But I still wanted the blessing of law enforcement, and I guess staying out of jail was a bit of a motivator as well.

I came with a printed list that they could distribute to their officers on duty. It had my name and title, our purpose, names of each team member and the cell number of each team leader, as we would break off into teams of four. I asked him if there were any hot spots in the city that we should avoid and also talked about where most of the homeless might congregate. At first, he was taken aback at the very idea that a pastor would even seek his advice or approval. He was also impressed that I had given him a list of names and contact numbers. If one of our teams called them, they would have a number and our back story, to know who they were dealing with. And we did have to call them.

Initiating a professional relationship with the police chief opened doors of permission and protection.

Please hear this out. This was not a Christian establishment; he was not a spiritual leader. The chief was simply a legal gatekeeper for the city. The police department was not concerned with our ministry effectiveness, yet they went out of their way to make sure we were doing okay.

It was midday, and the downtown park was getting busy with activity, mostly homeless coming to gather, much like we were doing. My team of four had been ministering to several different groups of people who were going through difficult times. From across the road, a very intoxicated woman came in our direction. She was yelling and cursing as she approached us. She was what I would regard as demonically influenced and not in a cooperative posture to receive ministry.

As she approached me, she began to yell out, "You are a man of God! I know why you are here!" This was repeated again and again, with slurred speech. She would not come close to me, but started to physically assault one of my younger female team members. It took the police about three minutes or less to respond.

The assailant had a list of warrants, and without any incident, the police quietly took her to a private room. As they were leaving, an officer took a look around to make sure we were safe and, with what appeared to be a nod of approval, left us to do our mission.

The honoring of this legal and civil authority opened doors to their hearts and caused them to pave a way for our mission outreach. We honored the gatekeeper, and the fruit of that work paid dividends, both in the natural and in the supernatural! When we do it God's way, we get God's results.

To the police, we were the good guys. We were on the side of the law, we were people downtown that they could trust and call on if needed. We were not a threat, a problem or a distraction. We helped the emotional state of the homeless for the days we were in town. The next time we came into town to pursue the same mission, they had a reference point to work from, and it was a good one. We walked their streets encouraging and praying for people. We bought people meals and even aided in catching a fugitive. We were on their good list.

Sometimes I wonder how differently the story would read if relational protocol had not preceded this outreach. Without a respectful approach priming the pump, I wonder just how each scenario would have played out in the end. Yes, ministry would have taken place, but how much more ministry will take place when operating under the favor of God? You see, God's favor on us is administered through men in authority, whether that authority is on the mission to reach the lost or if they are the lost. God can and will release His divine favor through them.

Looking at the life of Joseph, we can see the hand and favor of God being issued through the hands of the ungodly. Joseph was a slave, bought by Potiphar, an Egyptian officer of Pharaoh.

*³Now his master saw that the Lord was with him and how the Lord caused all that he did to prosper in his hand. ⁴So **Joseph** found **favor** in his sight and became his personal servant; and he made him overseer over his house, and all that he owned he put in his charge (Genesis 39:3-4).*

The favor of God continued to go with him, even in his state of slavery. We see that God's favor was delivered to him through men of a culture that did not believe in one true God. Even after he is wrongly accused and thrown in prison, God's favor comes through the favor of man.

*But the Lord was with **Joseph** and extended kindness to him, and gave him **favor** in the sight of the chief jailer (Genesis 39:21).*

[38] Then Pharaoh said to his servants, "Can we find a man like this, in whom is a divine spirit?" [39] So Pharaoh said to Joseph, "Since God has informed you of all this, there is no one so discerning and wise as you are. [40] You shall be over my house, and according to your command all my people shall do homage; only in the throne I will be greater than you." [41] Pharaoh said to Joseph, "See, I have set you over all the land of Egypt." [42] Then Pharaoh took off his signet ring from his hand and put it on Joseph's hand, and clothed him in garments of fine linen and put the gold necklace around his neck. [43] He had him ride in his second chariot; and they proclaimed before him, "Bow the knee!" And he set him over all the land of Egypt. [44] Moreover, Pharaoh said to Joseph, "Though I am Pharaoh, yet without your permission no one shall raise his hand or foot in all the land of Egypt." [45] Then Pharaoh named Joseph Zaphenath-paneah; and he gave him Asenath, the daughter of Potiphera priest of On, as his wife. And Joseph went forth over the land of Egypt (Genesis 41:38-45).

Not a recommended way to find a wife, but honoring civil authority sure worked for him.

This favor that God pours out to us through other vessels is there to make us succeed. He knows that, on our own, we can accomplish only so much, but when we are covered in His favor, we become exceedingly effective in our missions mandate. Walking out this favor will move us closer to saying, "Mission Accomplished."

Relational Ethics

Ministerial ethics can differ in its meaning, depending on the church structure you are familiar with, but there are Biblical foundations of ethics in ministry that should be a part of the missionary and every missions endeavor. Ethics in our relationships on and off the mission field should be a desire if reaching our missional goal is a priority to us.

When a ministry falls because of moral or financial failures, I propose to you that it all started with a betrayal of ethics. Let's look at the definition of the word:

eth·ics
1. a system of moral principles: the ethics of culture
2. the rules of conduct recognized in respect to a particular class of human actions or a particular group, culture, etc.: medical ethics; Christian ethics
3. moral principles, as of an individual: His ethics forbade betrayal of a confidence

Relational Keys

Deep Snow

Busting through mountain snowdrifts in the dark of night is both exhilarating and scary. I remember getting a call from a fellow minister, asking if I could assist him in ministry to a nearby village. I agreed to go and told him that I would meet him there with a small team later that evening. I needed a few hours to round up some team members and give plenty of time for that three-hour drive in the snow. Two hours into this venture, we could see that the snowdrifts were growing larger. My guess was that things would start to get a little better once we went over the pass, but the opposite was true. Lock and load! We were now using four-wheel drive with locked hubs, powering through deep snowdrifts. It was time to abort this mission and head back home, so that's what we did. We would later find out that the minister who drove in hours ahead of us followed behind the last snowplow that led him safely into the village. He told me, later, that he could see the road filling up with snowdrifts behind him as he climbed over the pass.

Often, we are unaware of the reasons things happen, but a few days later, I would find out the rest of the story. Someone called me from the village and said, "Glad you made it out safe; people were snowed in for a few days, until they could clear the roads." As I inquired how the services went, the answer was a lesson I needed to learn. "Actually, we didn't know that so-n-so was coming to the village. The person who invited him has not lived in the village for years, and she did not communicate with the leadership."

As it turned out, the ministry was not received well, and the services were a flop. The entry into the village was done without observing local protocol, and local authority was dishonored. When authority is dishonored, the hearts of the people remain closed. The person who did the inviting had the very best of intentions; they perceived a need in the village and thought that sending this other minster out there was a way to help serve that need. Good intentions don't generate great ministry results and never compensate for a lack of proper protocol.

Let me walk you through the three crucial mistakes that took place here.

1. The person who arranged this ministry event failed by not seeking permission from the established authority. By not pursuing an invitation from the spiritual leaders of that village, this event planner fueled a subversion of those in charge of the event.
2. The minister who was invited, and then in turn invited us to join, assumed that invitation had come from the top. He failed to ask some direct questions necessary to confirm that proper entry had been established. "What village leader is inviting us?" "Was this a desire of the village and/or church leadership?" "Do I have the approval of the chief or local pastor?"

3. Confirming the invitation before agreeing to come was never researched to see if the protocol had been followed. Likewise, I failed by walking in assumption that all was in order.

Assumption will birth dysfunction!

We have all heard it over and over again, "Never assume." And, unfortunately, it doesn't seem to sink in until we personally suffer the results of our assumptions.

The relational keys that we need to open up doors of opportunity cannot be copied, manufactured or bypassed just because we have a passion to get in there. We must honor the protocols that grant us the keys to the city.

Honor the protocols that grant you the keys to a culture!

Never assume, and always seek proper permission. It's God's way, and it works.

Making First Contact

Make sure your first contact is the right contact. When you first enter a new mission field, make sure the protocol has been followed and your intent to minister won't be tainted with an undermining spirit. Who invited you does make a difference. We would never think of showing up to a church service with intent to speak because someone in the congregation invited us. Wouldn't we feel much more secure if invited by the pastor? Yet, this happens far too often in the mission field.

Then, make sure your first contact remains your first

contact. There will always be someone who walks in "self-entitlement" but does not carry a legitimate authority. I've had people tell me that they are the spiritual gatekeeper of a community that they haven't lived in for three decades. Be careful who you align yourself with in the field. Utilize the intel from your lead trip, and make sure they are in good standing with the local government, spiritual leadership and local law enforcement.

Avoid any level of manipulation. One of the meanings of manipulation is "skillful or artful management." There are those who will adore your ministry with flattery; be aware of their personal agenda.

Honoring the actual authority of that area will bring alignment to your purpose and help your team avoid self-inflicted issues in the field.

Unsolicited Protection

It was midnight in late summer. With only a few hours of actual dark, we had been in a central park praying for people. The city has an ordinance that police strictly enforced, keeping people from sleeping in this central downtown park area. We had lost track of time while praying with people, and now two of the city's finest were making their sweep through the park, removing anyone that even looked like he might be thinking of staying in this public place. We were living with the homeless, so we started to head out and find a safe place under a bridge or at an abandoned parking lot, to get some street sleep. Like everyone on the street, this is always a challenge. Finding a safe place to sleep is actually shift work, with several power naps to get you through the night. By the time we had motioned to the other team to leave the park as well, an officer came over to me and said, "Your team can stay in the park. Nothing to worry about, have a great night." He was kind and professional, and his words were like a verbal pillow and blanket of comfort.

The city police department was not just supportive, they were accommodating our ministry work. They knew who we were, what our purpose was and, unlike most of the street people they work with, they had our cell numbers.

This unsolicited protection was given to our teams simply because we established relationship. The relational door was opened by a show of respect to the governing authority and paved the way for a successful mission.

Chapter Ten
The Follow-Through

His master said to him, "Well done, good and faithful slave. You were faithful with a few things, I will put you in charge of many things; enter into the joy of your master." (Matthew 25:21)

Building a Legacy

The year 2003 was the start of our organizing, training and taking mission teams on the Yukon River. We spent weeks each summer, traveling downriver, ministering to every village and fish camp we came into contact with. Often, the biggest challenge was just finding local people to talk with. We did it all, anything to draw a crowd. Much of it was successful. But not all of it. Trial and error was the process for finding better working methods of ministry in this region and unique culture.

We enjoyed six years of perfecting some of our

methods. But, in other areas, we were only surviving. We were seeing results in this remote region of Alaska, but with a limited timeframe of three weeks, there just had to be a better way to spend our time on the river.

"Why can't you stay longer?" was a common question asked by the locals. This question would come from all ages, but especially from the kids. We wanted to reach every community and village, but that kept us on the move and spread very thin. Just when we started to see some breakthrough in a village, it would be time to load the boats and get to the next village.

More than once we would have a child crawling on the boats with us, begging to come along, asking if we could take him or her home with us. These heart-wrenching moments would only feed our desires to stay longer. If only we could invest more time with the kids.

An elderly couple in one of the villages to which we traveled annually began to offer us the use of one of their properties on the river. "Pastor, you can use it to build a place for the kids."

This former village chief would continue to make this statement every summer. Then, in 2008, I sensed the leading of the Lord to take him up on his offer. We made plans to take a lead trip the next spring, assess the property, then come back the following month to build and run a camp for the youth of that area. This camp continues, to this day, to reach the young people of that region each summer with a message of hope (more on this camp later).

The Follow-Through

Consistency is a powerful tool that simply can't be replaced with any event.

We simply could not have built a camp right in the middle of these indigenous tribes without cultivating strong relationships, and cultivating relationships takes time. There is no way around it: Time must be invested into the lives of the people you want to reach before you can earn a voice. Creating a sustainable process of growing relationships in a mission field is crucial to its long-term effectiveness. I call this process "the follow-through."

fol·low-through:
1. the completion of a motion, as in the stroke of a tennis racket
2. the portion of such a motion after the ball has been hit
3. the act of continuing a plan, project, scheme or the like to its completion

Follow-through is very physical. It takes a proactive intent that moves with action. It cannot be achieved simply from roundtable discussion. One must do it.

Follow-through is a continuing of motion, even after impact. It keeps going on after the event.

Follow-through involves a plan of longevity, a detailed vision to see the larger goal accomplished.

From a panoramic view, follow-through is where evangelism meets discipleship. Without discipling taking place, the evangelism is usually wasted.

The Follow-Through Process

Here are a few steps that will help you maximize your short-term mission work and cultivate long-term residual ministry fruit.

All demographics:

Build long-term relationships with all age groups. It can be a great disadvantage if your relational energy is focused on one demographic. For example, only building relationship with the older group will shorten your long-term follow-up potential, obviously, because of that group's shorter remaining life span.

Focusing your relational investments on only the youth will limit your ability to build simply because they have not been granted the voice or position to embrace your ministry. It's important to build up relationship strength in each age group. This way, you will have the blessing of the elders and the teachable-ness of the children and every other possible scenario between the two. As you build closeness to each, unity will supernaturally be inspired, and a needed fusion will begin to take place in the age chasm.

Use Media

Utilize whatever social media is relevant to that community and culture. This is a great way to stay in regular contact when physical travel to them is not available. Multimedia is a great resource to keep your face in front of those living in the mission field.

Through live feeds where Internet is accessible and

sending video messages in a variety of formats to those who you desire to follow-up on, you can keep a continual injection of encouragement flowing their way. It's not uncommon in some villages of Alaska to find entire families living in 400-square-foot homes with no running water, no indoor plumbing and the only vehicle is a four-wheeler. Yet they have wireless Internet.

It's not about doing just one thing. Use all the media types you and your team find effective, and then make a media schedule to "plan out" your consistency. Literally, take a master calendar and schedule your calls, letters, e-mails, video calls, social media posts, audio and video messages, etc.

I recall getting a call from a leader in an Eskimo village more than two years after we had been there. He was requesting another shipment of the "encouragement CDs," as the youth (and many parents) had literally worn them out from so much use. To this day, we meet youth who tell us that they play those videos or audio recordings every day!

"Encouragement CD." Let me pass on this idea that was effective beyond our hopes. After the mission trip, while it was still fresh on our hearts, I gathered my staff and leaders into the studio, and we recorded encouraging messages. It was easy to fill an hour or more with short messages from each leader. We recorded the women speaking to the girls, and the men recorded words to the boys.

The content was a mix of scripture reading, verbal

teachings, power verses, relevant music and overall words of validation, encouragement and strength.

For more effectiveness, we tailor the final recording for a demographic or gender. For example, if we want to reach the teen girls, our female staff records specific messages that pertain to them.

Consistency

The "one-night stand" style of mission hurts all parties involved. A theme covered in the previous chapter of this book is that the missionary must "build lasting relationships."

This can only happen when the people you are ministering to remember your name and you remember theirs.

I'm a schedule guy. I like to keep the program going, to stay on track and keep true to the mission. But I learned the importance of "sitting down and listening." Now I make it a very important part of the mission to simply sip coffee and exchange stories.

This kind of long-term relational ministry is difficult to achieve without consistency. What does it mean to be consistent? Well, it's not a fixed number of visits in a month. It's simply about being constant to build on the work you started.

If you and your team are only able to visit a mission field annually, then be consistent with that. Build on projects and programs, but always focus on the people. Remain consistent year after year. Avoid the "one-night stand" style of ministry by first seeking the direction of the Lord as to where you should plant.

A farmer would not move to a new field each year and plant. The farmer knows that it takes time to see a healthy crop growing and years for a mature harvest to develop.

He also knows that the crop will get better each year as he improves the quality of the ground through his investments of blood, sweat and tears. The farmer's faithfulness to his field will one day pay self-sustaining dividends.

The team that bounces around the globe, making quick relational investments, is often using missions as their excuse to travel the globe.

At the very least, this robs their potential of a much healthier harvest.

WX

Winter Xtreme is a winter youth camp that we provide in the local area. Imagine snow volleyball, sledding, snow hockey and dog mushing all taking place in the same arctic camp environment. That is WX! The 14th year of this camp was in the early months of 2014.

The longevity of this youth event has been nothing less than epic. With the same "destiny" theme each year, we have been blessed to see hundreds of youth connect with their purpose and step onto their destiny road. Many of the ministry staff we are now blessed with were once youth attending this camp. Years ago, they attended, and now they run it!

When I see the many youth who are now grown and fully engaged in ministry, I'm thankful to the Lord. These many blessings would not have come to pass without a heart for longevity and a commitment to consistency. This annual event creates an environment where life-changing God encounters can take place in the lives of this generation.

So find the direction of the Lord, make a long-term commitment, dig your boots in deep and plant a harvest of consistency!

Mission longevity will yield a sustaining harvest.

Honor Local Leaders

The way you stay in contact with the people of a mission field will either honor or dishonor the local spiritual leader(s). I understand that not every community or region that you and I are called to actually has a local pastor, elder, spiritual leader, etc. But, in most any culture, you can find the recognized leader. Maybe they are a political leader or possibly a tribal/clan overseer. No matter the actual title. If this person or these persons fill that role for their people, then it's imperative that they be treated with honor.

Always speak to the local people through that leader. Be careful not to undermine the local authority simply because you were better received by someone else in that community. Become the missionary team that local leadership can count on.

Take ownership in that mission field. Find their local

vision, and come alongside to help them reach it! Embrace the prophetic call that God put on that leader for that culture of people, rather than marching into the field with your own agenda.

Mission's Evaluation

If this mandate to do the Great Commission is the most important thing in life (which it is), then refining our effectiveness through continual evaluation should become a regular part of the total mission's program.

Schedule a time of "debriefing" for your team, after the mission. Evaluate your relational and logistical success while it's fresh in your minds. Gather input both collectively and individually. Plan a short "exit interview" for each team member. Often, important details and information will be brought to your attention in this more private setting. As a leader over many missions endeavors, I have experienced amazing insight during these times of debriefing.

When you oversee the big picture, it's alarming just how many things take place that you didn't see. There is a natural tendency for the leader to be focused on the flight home instead of these details. That kind of tunnel vision can look right over areas that could have been adjusted in the field. A more favorable debrief can be encouraged by having proper leadership assistance and ministry assignments, as mentioned in Chapter Seven.

This time of evaluation not only serves to measure the depth and width of your relationship building, but also provides a great opportunity to discuss the most productive methods of follow-through for those who were ministered to. This can also be a time to share the basic vision of your follow-through campaign and get the team excited about the ministry after the mission.

When leaders provide an environment where their leadership can be evaluated, not only will they have a great opportunity to see their weak areas and strengths, team members will also see a much-needed example of humility. This humility will encourage a transparency within the team and an openness, creating a new level of trust. It can bring inner healing to all involved. When that chasm of "us and them" is broken down, a new level of unity will be cultivated for the next mission mandate.

Use What Works

Sustaining a growing missionary work is created by providing opportunities for relational longevity in that field. There is no "one thing" that works best with every culture. I have found that the answer is in doing it all. If it gives you an open door to meet someone, reach someone or teach someone, do it! And do it with lasting intent.

Leaders Create a Screen

This nugget of wisdom should be understood before we cover the follow-up methods. I would recommend that mission team leaders develop a "screening" process for restricting relational contact to those ministered to in the mission field.

The Follow-Through

Unfortunately, we will often have individuals on a mission team who are driven more by their hormones than by the Holy Spirit. These "horny-mones" will inspire unproductive contact with people, bring discouragement to that local leader and promote a negative view of the entire missionary team. Because this inappropriate contact is usually done privately, through social media, we discourage team members who have not been screened from exchanging their personal information with locals. I have been known to put a member on a plane and send him or her home when they have proven unteachable in this area.

The method of your screening process will differ depending on the demographic and structure of your team. One of the purposes of this book is to encourage "all" followers of Jesus to get busy doing their part in this mission to reach the lost. So I'm not implying that we screen out every potential team member.

For those who love the people of the mission we are serving, we must be aware of the wonderful potential of follow-up, as well as the undermining damage the enemy can do through "missionaries" who have some tainted relational motives. Yes, follow-up contact is necessary. But use wisdom regarding who you allow to do it.

There are two principles that, if followed, will very effectively filter out the enemy's ability to infect a relationship:

- <u>Keep all contact the same gender</u>. This guideline is very helpful in protecting the integrity of the mission and will keep the majority of inappropriate contact from taking place.
- <u>Involve a third-party person</u>. This powerful method is actually used frequently in the business world. While the professional purpose in the third-party communication may be intended to keep all information clear and open the door for professional accountability to a given task, it also serves to keep any ill motives from developing in the personal correspondence.

Although the "same gender" principle will definitely help you avoid most dysfunction, in today's culture, misunderstandings and relational confusion are a real potential even within same-sex contact.

Let me give some examples:

One of our staff had connected with a young man from one of our village mission outreaches. This young man was open to discipleship and personal ministry. The phone calls from this teen increased, and the text messages became less about the ministry to him and more personally driven. After digging a little deeper, he confessed that he was sexually abused by a man as a young boy and that this had influenced him into a bisexual lifestyle. The demonic influence on this young man's life was infecting his motives toward this staff member, as well as his ability to open up for healing.

Another example:

She was young when a family member started sexually abusing her. She responded positively to one of our youth camps, and one of our female leaders started meeting with her and speaking about her life.

As this ministry relationship developed, however, it became apparent that this young teen was sexually attracted to her spiritual guide.

Many more stories can be told of those going to the mission field struggling with the same past abuse and sexual temptation.

Clarity, transparency and accountability have always been protective strengths in any ministry relationship. But never have they been more needed than in the culture we now live in.

These unhealthy connections usually will start in the field and, like bacteria, grow in the dark through private contacts. Much of this can be avoided by better screening the motives of a team member and keeping a mission schedule free from unnecessary free time.

It's not uncommon to find someone on the mission team who is focused on his or her own mission. During scheduled times of prayer preparation, as mentioned in Chapter Three, a unified passion of combating the enemy can be developed, rather than a passion for batting eyelashes.

MISSION ACCOMPLISHED

It was the 1980s, and we had a large team going to Mexico. This was a 10-day mission, and the team was excited to get going. On the first day of the outreach, it became apparent that one of our adult team members was on this mission to find a wife!

I'm not saying I perceived this was his intent. He actually announced it: "I'm looking for a wife, and that is why I am here." He spoke this with confidence, as if God had told him to join us for this purpose.

Well, he must have missed the voice of God on this one, because he not only came home wifeless, he was a complete distraction to the mission. His self-centered focus did not benefit the team's unity.

Make it clear to the team that all mission and follow-up contact is for evangelism and discipleship, not for hunting down a spouse. We want to encourage people to step into these mission opportunities, as well as build strong mentoring relationships that lean toward discipleship. In doing this, implementing methods that set them up for success is imperative.

Here are some of the methods you may want to add to your follow-up campaign:

Personal Visits

Whether your mission field is a town, city, neighborhood or village, the personal face-to-face visit is tough to beat. Depending on the culture, the personal contact you may want to use will differ. For example, here in bush Alaska, we will modify our personal touch in alignment with that protocol.

In some communities, a small team making home visits is very much appreciated, while in other Native communities, we find that offering a public event better fits their style of introduction. As we covered in Chapter Eight, learn the way that they connect within their protocol. Once that initial connection is made, building on those relationships should be part of your primary mission goal.

Live Video Calls

Second only to the face-to-face visit, video calls are very personable and keep both parties from "checking out" during a conversation. Have you ever called someone and found yourself repeating your words because the other person's video game was distracting them? Video calls keep the attention of both sides on the screen.

Scheduling video calls with groups of people whenever you can is a wonderful way to make eye contact. Start promoting these special times in advance so that they have time to gather people on their end. These can become effective times of encouragement, as well as discipleship.

Phone Calls

If calls can be made to that community, call them, and call regularly! Make a calling schedule, which ties in with all the other scheduled communications to those in that mission field. Never underestimate the power of the voice. Depending on the culture and technological availability, a phone call may or may not be an option. But when it is, use it!

Written forms of communication are wonderful, but they lack that human inflection in a person's voice. On the phone is an excellent time to pray for someone, as well as developing the long-term relationship.

Use phone features available to you, like three-way calling or conference calls. Using the speaker phone mode with that third-party person in the room is a good habit to establish.

Connect Cards

These are great tools that can be used in a variety of venues, especially if designed correctly. The connect card is typically larger than a business card, but smaller than a postcard. These are effective to hand out personally in the field, and because of the design, they are great to leave in public places as well.

Unlike a business card, it's best to not have personal phone numbers or e-mails of those on the team listed on a connect card. Rather, show contact information for reaching the church, mission director or those assigned for follow-up contact.

Like the postcard, a photo, relevant to that outreach, helps people to make a memory connection. A group picture of the team is also a great idea.

Postcards

Personalize postcards with photos taken from your mission field. These photos are great reminders, and the postcard is inexpensive to print and mail. Although people are more apt to get their mail via computer, "snail mail" still has its place. People of all ages still enjoy the personal touch of receiving special mail.

One of the nice advantages of using postcards is that they take minimal time to process, which makes them a method that can be repeated over and over. We design several different cards and have those available to staff and mission team members at our follow-up/debriefing meeting.

Moreover, we actually schedule a time to write personal notes to those to whom we ministered and schedule the mailing of these cards. Several cards would be written from several team members. So a staggered schedule would be put on a calendar, keeping a consistent flow of encouraging contact.

Door Hanger Invitations

Nothing can replace the one-on-one personal connection, but a well-designed invitation can be a great tool that has lasting payoff when no one is home.

I recall an outreach to a small town in Northern California. The local pastor wanted to make his church and ministry available to a community that seemed to be blind to the church's facilities and services.

The pastor was willing to make changes in his

methods, but needed to get the word out with a minimal budget.

I had a young, energetic team ready to take a mountain, which was helpful since we knocked on every door in the city of Mount Shasta.

Our canvassing had a threefold purpose: personally invite people to some special services, offer prayer over any family needs and leave a door hanger invitation if no one was home.

Let's talk about the invitation. Never put a date on a flyer that is not personally handed to someone. No one likes to read about an event he or she missed, since it's old news as soon as that event or service has started. We handed out event invitations to those we personally spoke to, but the invitation left hanging on the doorknobs was designed to be ageless.

The door hanger should not be overly wordy. It should be printed in a natural handwriting style or current attractive font, a professional layout by someone actually gifted at design. Keep the door hanger/flyer focused on their needs, and invite them to come next Sunday or "call us for prayer."

One of the benefits of the timeless flyer is that God can use it long after it has been left at a home or office. Often weeks, months and even years later, a person will come across this invitation and be compelled to respond.

One pastor told me this story: "A year after your team had left a door hanger at a home in our city, the wife found it behind her sofa while spring cleaning. The timing was just right for her, as she was dying inside and needed answers. She and her family came the next Sunday and received the love and forgiveness of Jesus!"

If that flyer or invitation was event driven, with a fixed date, then the printed message would have been much less personal and connecting. The attraction is highly increased when the invitation stays relevant over time. It's human nature to not attach ourselves to past events.

Let me explain a little further. I once had a few hundred t-shirts printed up that promoted "90 Years of Missions" in our state. People were eating them up. I thought that the concept was brilliant! It seemed as if everyone wanted one during the event.

As soon as year 91 began, however, these shirts could only be given away. I obviously needed a class in marketing. My favorite sweatshirt is a camouflage hoodie that reads, "Cabela's Since 1961." It's my favorite for several reasons: 1) it's Cabela's; 2) it's camo; 3) I was also born in 1961; 4) its statement stays relevant from year to year; it never gets old.

Modern missionary teams usually engage in short-term missions trips. These short-term blocks of time need to be impactful. The door hanger and personal/printed invitations find better long-term effectiveness if they point to an existing ministry in that area. That existing ministry can sustain spiritual growth, rather than simply promote a one-time event.

The focus here is the local pastor, missionary, spiritual leader, etc. Without the stability of a person who continues personal ministry to the people, the invitation serves little purpose.

Do door hangers still work? I do think they can be helpful in making connection with people if the purpose of the printed invitation has a purpose of personal follow-up.

Here is a recap of the invitational door hanger:

1. Local direction: Make sure you have a local spiritual leader who can receive, invest and grow the people that will respond to this invite.
2. Keep it neutral: If you need to promote an event, put that on a separate flyer. Make it look like a flyer: flashy and fun! But make the invitation look personal, inviting and non-dated. This will give it the potential of being relevant and effective long after its placement.
3. Plan follow-up: Return to your home church or business with the intent to stay connected. The invitation is a great conversation starter: "Did you get the note I left you?"

Missions Embedded

Reluctant to go? Yes, I was, too. Not out of fear, but because I understood the cost. I'm not talking about the monetary cost. I was thinking about the mental and spiritual commitment it would take if I agreed to go.

THE FOLLOW-THROUGH

"You should take your team to Minto!" was a statement I heard for three years. It really got old as person after person would make this suggestion. Being one of the only villages that is on a dirt road system, it seemed as if everybody and their dog went to Minto with a mission team. I kept my focus on other locations, villages that were more remote and that I had never heard people talking about. I really didn't want to make a trip to any village until I could do it right.

God spoke very clearly to me concerning it. He made it clear that, if I went, I needed to make a "long-term" commitment to these people. I needed to make constant visits, building lasting relationships, rather than just visit and check it off my village missions list. It was July of 2001 when I agreed to go meet the people of Minto and get a lay of the land. It turned out to be a mission lead trip that keeps me frequenting that village to this day.

Spending time and being consistent moves you to a level of ministry relationship that is more like a family. My family and team spent many Christmases in Minto, countless hours fellowshipping and ministering to all ages. We continue to invest in the new generation as they sprout up.

The influence and voice that the missionary is given through longevity is priceless. This ministry influence grows to a greater level as more history is being made, thereby developing more trust. Minto is not a place we go to do mission work. This is a village into which we are embedded!

MISSION ACCOMPLISHED

The short-term mission trip can be powerfully effective. Effective mission work is not just about staying longer; it's about going more often. Never underestimate the potential of a well-trained team going into a region that is foreign to them and finding God's favor as they are used to reach the lost.

Remember, they are *His* lost, in *His* fields. God is calling us to those fields. Let's go there, and go there often!

Chapter Eleven
The Payoff

*For just as the body without the spirit is dead,
so also faith without works is dead. (James 2:26)*

Faith in Action

Those airplanes looked so beautiful to us. That well-seasoned old Navajo and even the older Cessna 180 looked like private jets to me when they landed.

It was 1999, and instead of preparing for Y2K, I was preparing to take a team of youths into a remote Eskimo village. I had been preparing this young team for several months, and now, just days before we were to head out on this mission, it was definitely crunch time. It was a huge challenge: packing enough food and ministry supplies to last the duration for this team while making sure that it all stayed under the weight restrictions for a flight.

Two days before our departure, we were hard at work sealing boxes and weighing supplies in the staging area. It was then that I received this call: "The plane scheduled to pick up your team has been grounded for maintenance. Sorry about that."

Really?! Wow! No plane? But the call to this mission was so strong and clear to me, I simply could not accept this meant not going.

I quickly got on the phone and started making calls. After several hours of calling, a connection was finally made, and we had another pilot and a plane large enough lined up to transport this team.

It was the evening before we were to leave, and the 8 a.m. flight was the focus of our last-minute packing. The team was excited and energized!

Then the phone rang. "Hey, Pastor, gonna need to cancel flying you in the morning because flight annuals are grounding my plane." Grounded!? My goodness! I hadn't seen so much grounding since junior high!

I went into the next room and gave the update to the entire team. I repeated what the pilot had said, and I reminded them of what God had said. The more I spoke out the vision and reminded the team of all the great things that God had provided thus far, the more our faith was being built up. You could actually feel the faith increase in the room.

"God called us to this mission, and we will be standing on that runway ready to fly at 8 a.m. sharp! We may not have a plane, but God does! We may not know how this can work, but God does! This was His plan, and He will make a way! Are you with me?!"

We were pumped, excited and believing that God would come through for us.

It was about 11 p.m. when this call came into the office:

Caller: *Are you the pastor taking a team into Shaktoolik?*

Me: *I sure am.*

Caller: *I got a call from a guy who got a call from another pilot saying that you all needed to fly in the morning, is that right?*

Me: *You got that right! What size plane do you have?*

Caller: *We're flying a Navajo, but it looks like you will need more room, so I have a larger second plane lined up, hauling mail to that same village, if you are interested.*

Now, only seven hours until we were to pull out of the driveway, I sure did have some great news for the team. I found them right where I had left them, fervently crying out to God for a flight. I can't describe the emotion in that room that night. This young team had just experienced the hand of God moved by their intense prayer. Their faith was on steroids!

Had everything moved along smoothly, I'm convinced that we would have prayed less. Father God wanted to do a mighty work through us in that village, and He knew that we needed our faith to be on fire for that to happen. Our extreme need positioned us for extreme intercession.

I've learned through that situation and many others

like it that the challenges of missions are there to activate our faith. Sometimes we actually need our situation to get disastrous so that we will get desperate and cry out for the hand of the Lord.

Let Father God be the super in the middle of your natural.

There was the temptation to give up. Even the senior pastor was telling me that maybe we needed to postpone the trip, it just wasn't working out. Any time we make decisions based on the logical or natural, we receive the results of the logical and the natural. Postponing would have taught this team to make decisions from fear, not faith. I understand that there are those times when God directs us to postpone a given mission, and He often reveals the purpose and advantage of that delay later. Even in that circumstance, however, we need to involve our faith. This step of faith we took activated the miracle that we needed, and that miracle "super charged" our faith. And the increased faith activated many more supernatural moves of God in the village. The most effective missions are drenched in the supernatural.

Mission Accomplished

Mission work is a wonderful place to see God move in your team, both personally and collectively. Why wouldn't God want to do amazing things in the hearts of the missionary? Remember, it's His plan, His purpose and His design, and He wants us to accomplish this mission. He knows that we need a Holy Spirit encounter so we can pass it on. God knows that if we only experience "information" about Him, that is all our mission will take to the lost and hurting. But if we experience a powerful healing impartation from the Lord, God knows we will take that with us on our mission.

No Acceptable Losses

Finding success in doing the Great Commission should be our complete priority as followers of Jesus. It's sad that some of us get more upset when our football team fumbles a game than when our mission trip fumbles a chance to reach the lost. Games are designed to have a loser, but mission work was designed to find success every time. In sports there are "acceptable losses," but this mindset should never enter the mind or heart of the minister. If it's your son or daughter who is lost, that's simply not an "acceptable loss"!

When we are on a mission to reach the lost kids of God, failure should never be attributed to our sloppy ministry. The greatest preparation yields the greatest return.

Winter Wonderland

We sent out posters to the surrounding villages months earlier. The village of Selawik would be the location for the winter youth camp our team would be providing. Youths came from villages all over the region, and some even traveled by snow machine (snowmobile, for you non-Alaskans) 150 miles one way in the snow to attend this camp. As the small chartered aircraft landed on the runway made of snow, we were transported by snow machine and dog teams to the church we would call home for four days.

The days were filled with relational workshops, and the nights were dominated by long, powerful youth rallies. Young people were responding to the presence of the Holy Spirit and rushing to the front each night for prayer. We were overwhelmed at the openness and deliverance that was taking place on a mass scale.

This village and region had experienced the pain of one suicide a month, and they were desperate for God to intervene. I received a call from the village two weeks after the event, telling us of a tragic accident: A teen girl was crossing the river and broke through the ice. The one giving this difficult report had a sound of relief, as she said this youth had been at our camp, had given her life to Jesus and was completely changed.

Three years later, leaders from the region informed me that there had not been one suicide since our ministry in the village.

God is faithful to honor and anoint our obedience in faith.

The Payoff

One of the wonderful payoffs of missions is seeing lives be transformed. Not just the people group that you are reaching, but also those who are doing the reaching.

The Word of God is clear concerning the importance of spreading the Gospel. No matter what your heavenly assignment is, you are called to advance the mission of the Great Commission. When this life-changing message of the cross hits the hearts of the lost, their lives are transformed for eternity. As spoken in Romans 10:15, *How will they preach unless they are sent? Just as it is written, How beautiful are the feet of those who bring good news of good things!* We know that the one receiving the ministry is blessed, but this is referring to the blessing reserved for the one bringing the life-altering message.

Whether you are leading a mission team or joining one, let's take a look at a few of the payoffs that take place in missionary work:

1) Lives Transformed

As mentioned above, not just those that your mission is reaching, but also each member of that team is subjected to transformation. There are greater levels of revelation that can only take place when boots hit the ground. You can hear about missions, or study the history of missions, but nothing will replace going on a mission trip, short-term or long-term. The impartation that takes place in the field is unique and simply not replaceable.

When a team member returns from a legitimate mission experience, their involvement and effectiveness will be altered in a positive way. As covered in Chapter One of this book, I use the word "legitimate" in reference to participating in an actual mission's outreach or event, rather than a trip simply based on personal entertainment camouflaged behind a mission's label.

When the "mission" becomes a part of them, they take it off the field and into their community. Some of these team members will actually think that they can do mission work in their own town, city and communities.

Yes! That once "good-hearted pew warmer" returns home discontent with simply filling a seat in the church. They desire to proactively get busy with their mission mandate.

2) Leaders Encouraged

Show me a ministry leader that doesn't need encouragement. A mission endeavor could be just the ticket! It's during those times of grinding ministry schedules that a pastor or spiritual leader often needs a shot in the arm. Especially when you see that your church or ministry has hit a plateau. That could be the perfect time to plan a mission trip.

You might say, "We really don't have the funds for that right now." And you probably don't. It's in those times of real need that the hand of God shows up. It's in those times of lack that Jesus pours out provision. That miraculous provision comes from the cries of God's people, igniting their faith to fulfill His command.

Need a jumpstart? Plan a mission trip. Need some encouragement? Plan a mission trip. Need your pew warmers to become church builders? Plan a mission trip. Need to get your church to the next level? Plan a mission trip! I think you get the point. The temptation to wait for all the stars and planets to line up will only delay your corporate destiny.

3) Hearts Called

Like many of you, I have a personal story of responding to an altar call and hearing a distinct call to ministry. Maybe you were at a summer youth camp when the Lord spoke clearly to you. Thank God He still does that!

He calls us for His kingdom purpose. Father God has no limits or restrictions, and He can call us from out of our sleep. He will even knock us off our journey of self-agenda, much like He did with Saul in Acts 9. I must say that in all my ministry experience (starting in 1982), I have never seen more people called into their kingdom destiny than when they are on the mission field. It seems that being in the middle of active missionary work conditions the heart for receiving the spiritual ears to hear the voice of the Lord more clearly.

Do you want to see people called into their God-given ministry purpose? Then help them get their mission activated!

4) Destiny Found

We see in the first chapter of Jeremiah the Lord speaking to a young person:

⁴Now the word of the Lord came to me saying, ⁵"Before I formed you in the womb I knew you, and before you were born I consecrated you; I have appointed you a prophet to the nations." ⁶Then I said, "Alas, Lord God! Behold, I do not know how to speak, because I am a youth." ⁷But the Lord said to me, "Do not say, 'I am a youth,' because everywhere I send you, you shall go, and all that I command you, you shall speak. ⁸Do not be afraid of them, for I am with you to deliver you," declares the Lord. ⁹Then the Lord stretched out His hand and touched my mouth, and the Lord said to me, "Behold, I have put My words in your mouth. ¹⁰See, I have appointed you this day over the nations and over the kingdoms, to pluck up and to break down, to destroy and to overthrow, to build and to plant" (Jeremiah 1:4-10).

Are you getting this? God is saying to us, "Before I formed you in the womb, I knew you." God actually had some hands-on involvement in forming you. I recall having a personal revelation while reading this passage.

I was so amazed that God, our Creator, would actually get personally involved in our design. He is not a distant God. Rather, He is interested in our every little detail because He created all of them. This amazing uniqueness was designed into us so we will have the direction to do the last part of verse 10 — " build and plant."

In sincere curiosity, I asked the Lord this question: "Lord, what were You doing in my mother's womb?"

Without any hesitation, I heard this answer, loud and clear: "Planting seeds of destiny."

Those four words would forever change my life! God's answer brought insight and understanding into so much of the scripture for me. From then on, when I would hear statements about God's hand, I would have a very personal view of that phrase because with His hands He was planting seeds of my destiny. And He uniquely did this for you as well.

Those seeds of destiny must be brought to life with our faith in action. When we take steps of faith, we infuse these seeds with our obedience. Then, God pours out His anointing, and we see supernatural growth.

Big Opening

With a handkerchief over his mouth and nose, my boating assistant was lying down on the bow of the boat, spotting for a clear path on the water. Through the thick smoke, we could see the flames on each side of the river. In those early days, the advantage of using a GPS was not an option for us as it is today. The Yukon River had not seen a wildfire of this magnitude for decades, and here I was, leading a large young mission team into what appeared to be an endless cloud of smoke.

The other boat pilots were forced to run in single file behind me and rather close to each other as we were moving slowly in this wall of darkness. The visibility worsened as we headed farther down the mighty Yukon. Navigating the lead boat on a hope and a prayer, I desperately needed to get this fleet of boats to the next village.

Was I concerned? Definitely, and for several reasons.

Will we run into a sandbar or an island? Will we find the village or slowly motor past it? Can we find a camping area that is safe from fire and smoke? Will the team hold up physically? I knew this was affecting everyone's respiratory system, energy and spirits.

Actually, I was unaware that one of the students on this trip had been struggling with his breathing for days. Not wanting to get sent home while in the last village, he kept his condition a private matter.

We managed to keep in the north channel and found our way to the next village. The island was only 200 yards from the village bank and would make a safe camping area. After setting up, one of my staff came running to me. "Jeremiah is not breathing!"

We ran to his tent and found him curled up with no sign of breathing. We carried him to the river and set him up on the bow of a boat. He then began to breathe again and said he would be fine. I told him to stay there, breathe slowly and regain his strength. I needed time to formulate a plan, as this was a new one for me. (After this event, I began keeping a satellite phone with me at all times.)

We kept a close eye on him, and he appeared to be recovering, or so I thought. Moments later, I looked up, and he was gone! I ran, yelling for him, but no one had seen him leave the boat. As I approached it, I found him on the floor of the boat gasping for air!

Dan, Tim, Omar and I quickly pushed the boat out and hurried across to the other side of the river. As we approached, a woman was down at the landing on her four-wheeler. We yelled and told the woman, a health aide as it turned out, that we needed help to get to the clinic. After getting him uphill to the clinic, we laid him on the medical bed. I asked her to call for a medical evacuation ASAP.

She was not sure what to do. It wasn't because of a lack of experience or concern, but because of new clinic policy. She began to tell me her situation.

Only minutes before we approached her at the riverbank, she had flown back to the village from the city. She had been to a Native-sponsored medical training workshop, a workshop that stressed the importance of "non-Natives not receiving medical assistance from a village clinic"! Here she was, only home a few minutes (with this new training), and along comes a non-Native in need of medical care.

Jeremiah is about as non-Native Indian as you can get. He's not just white. He's "honky white." And here was this young man, dying in her facility.

She called and even begged the dispatcher of the medical flight service to send out a plane. All aircraft were grounded because of the wildfires and dangerous lack of visibility. While all the phone calling was going on, locals had picked up on our radio communication from the clinic to the island, and people were gathering around outside, some waiting and others praying. He still had a pulse, but he was not breathing.

The team back at the camp was in deep intercession, and the men who were with me watching Jeremiah were also praying aggressively. "No pulse!" they said as I leaned over him. This facility did not have the equipment or personnel for this stage of crisis.

I was so mad! Here we are, on a mission trip, and one of my team is going to die in the village?! The praying increased, and with a burst of anger, I grabbed a towel that was soaked in cold water and slapped his chest with it like a sledgehammer. His body jarred to life, and he started breathing!

Later, the health aide asked me how I knew to do that, as if it was some secret procedure for waking up the dead. It was said later that I may have started some new back-up plan for clinics. "If all else fails, hammer them in the chest with a big, cold, wet towel."

The health aide finally convinced a medical team to fly in our direction, a flight of about 100 miles north from Fairbanks. As the medical transport, with the EMTs, approached the village, they had no view of the village airstrip. The entire village and surrounding area was encased in a wall of rust-colored smoke. Just as they were aborting the mission, suddenly, right below them, a hole in the cloud of smoke opened up and gave the pilot a clear view of the airstrip on which to land.

Jeremiah was breathing just enough to survive, and we wasted no time loading him onto that plane. We knew that God had His hand on the situation and could see it confirmed before our eyes. As the plane ascended through that open tunnel in the smoke, we watched the smoke close off behind them. They made it safely out and transported Jeremiah to the hospital, in spite of the growing fires and the smoke increasing through the airways.

Standing on that village airstrip, I looked around and saw the same look of relief on the faces of my team. We headed back to the camp because we had ministry to do. We had a mandate to follow, and we knew from past experiences, God would work this mess to our good.

And we know that God causes all things to work together for good to those who love God, to those who are called according to His purpose (Romans 8:28).

If we fulfill those two conditions, then there is nothing to worry about. We know that we are called to His purpose.

The question then remains, do we really love God?

If you love Me, *you will keep My commandments (John 14:15).*

Oh, whatever happened to that young man on our team? In October of 2006, I overloaded a boat with Jeremiah and all his belongings. We launched into the Yukon River and headed the 90 miles downriver to the remote Native village of Fort Yukon. He became the pastor over that same region, where he had almost died two years earlier.

Pastor Jeremiah Niemuth and his wife, Sharnay, continue this long-term missionary work in that region as Assembly of God U.S. Missionaries to this day.

- Invest your faith into the God who gave you the vision.
- Invest your resources into the mission.
- Invest your heart and time into the people.

It may be hard, but the payoff is well worth it.

Chapter Twelve
Qualifications

Fight the good fight of faith; take hold of the eternal life to which you were called, and you made the good confession in the presence of many witnesses.
(1 Timothy 6:12)

High and Dry

Visibility was getting difficult, and the boat pilot was getting a little too cocky. But the load was moderate, the jet unit was running excellently and the river was like glass. This was a great time to run the shallows on the south side of the massive Yukon River.

The local chief had asked if we could deliver some mail to an elder and her family, downriver at her family's fish camp. We agreed and headed out onto the mighty river with a box of mail and some eager hearts to minister.

Fish camps are a great place to do some productive and relational ministry. It's on local turf, but you have a captive audience. After campfire tea, smoked salmon and some great ministry, we needed to beat the storm and get back upriver to our camp, before darkness made it dangerous to navigate.

The Yukon River is not a place on which you want to get your boat stuck. Moreover, this river gives you more opportunities to be stupid than you could imagine. And more experience does not always correlate with more wisdom. Sometimes the less-experienced boat pilot will take fewer chances than the one who might be a tad overconfident. Things were going just fine on our upriver trek until those big long shallows on the south side started growing.

Weaving in and out of the many sandbars was exhilarating. But then it happened: a bottleneck! We had run out of options to turn around, and we were committed to attempt passage through this bottleneck, which was about 200 yards of narrowing, shallow water and two long gravel bars on each side. The farther we went into it, the more we were sure of our imminent demise. The crashing noise of rocks scraping the bottom of the boat echoed across the river. We came to a scratching stop only 50 yards from the exit that would have brought deeper waters. Great!

Here we were, stuck high and dry, in the middle of the Yukon River. The two miles downriver from camp might as well have been a hundred. I grabbed the two-way radio from the dashboard, only to find that it was dead. I took the batteries out, gave them a good massage, reinstalled them and found enough juice to turn it on. "Send a boat downriver! We're stuck! Send a boat downriver!" was all I could get transmitted into the airways before the batteries flat-lined.

Well, Mr. Jet-Boat Pilot, it's time to face the music. So I turned around and began a heartfelt repenting to my small crew who looked like a bunch of angry pirates ready to be rid of their idiotic leader. Yes, that cocky, overconfident, thrill-seeking, seasoned river captain was yours truly — me.

Are you qualified to lead others on a mission trip?

After hearing this story, you may not think I'm qualified to lead a mission team. Well, after living out so many of these stories, I'm inclined to agree with you. Yes, you will make mistakes. But as you learn from each one, you will find yourself making far fewer of them. Mission work should be successful. It's all about reaching God's sons and daughters with the saving power of the Cross. It was God's idea, His plan, and He wants us to be a success at obeying Matthew 28.

The Great Commission is our mission, and we are the missionaries who are qualified by the work of the Cross to be successful at reaching the lost. As you have heard before, "God doesn't call the qualified. He qualifies the called."

Wall or Speed Bump?

His ride was a "low-rider," and it was lowered about as low as you could go. It was 1977, Southern California, and the local high school was joining the growing trend of adding speed bumps in the parking lots. I think you know where this is going.

With big, fluffy dice dangling from the rearview mirror, glistening chrome and Latino tunes thumping from the windows, that Chevy high-centered on a speed bump, which temporarily stopped all forward movement. Then, several embarrassed young men exited the giant teeter-totter. Sorry, you YouTubers, but there were no smart phones back in the day. (Hey, ask your grandpa to explain what a phone booth looked like.) This massive car that far outweighed the speed bump had plenty of power to get where it needed to go. But its physical posture had been altered. Its perspective had been lowered so much that even a little bump could stop it. At that time, and at that moment, that little "mole hill" might as well have been a mountain.

Often, the wall that appears to stand in the way of our vision is nothing more than a mole hill. That little bump can appear devastating if our perspective has been influenced to a low perspective. If we see ourselves through a filter of lies, induced by the father of lies, then a lowly little bump can hang us up and keep us from vital forward movement.

Canceling the lies of the enemy that keep us from our

mission's destiny is only a prayer away. It's truly amazing just how much of our lives can be stifled by lies when in just a few moments, we can be freed from those life-altering falsehoods.

*⁵Thomas said to Him, "Lord, we do not know where You are going, how do we know the way?" ⁶Jesus said to him, "I am the **way**, and the **truth**, and the **life**; no one comes to the Father but through Me (John 14:5-6).*

Jesus is the WAY, the TRUTH and the LIFE. In this single sentence, Jesus was giving us the way to use truth to free our life.

Earlier in John 8:32, Jesus says: *And you will know the **truth**, and the **truth** will make you **free**.*

You see, the most effective way to counter a lie is by revealing the truth. What lies are keeping you emotionally captive? Often, we live by a lie and don't even know it. Things that have been said from years ago that we slowly embraced, such as, "You will never amount to anything." I remember a teacher who was handing out report cards in grade school, publicly tell me that I was stupid. Without any conscious effort on my part, I began to live by that lie. I recall bringing home a report card and reluctantly handing it to my mom. At the top was a nickname, given to me by my teacher, clearly handwritten: "Ronald D. Bratt."

Even at this young age, I had heard enough whispers of the enemy that these words were as good as truth to me. Unknowingly, I had come fully into agreement with these verbal contracts on my life. I was well into adulthood before I asked Jesus to expose the lies that kept my potential in chains and to reveal to me His truth.

It might have been a lie formed from the absence of something that should have been said, like, "I love you!" "I believe in you!" or "You are important to me." The enemy will use a time of trauma, loss or abuse to plant and reinforce these lies.

What lie is keeping you down? What view of you is influenced by a lie? When we start to believe a lie, we have empowered its destructive deception.

"I'm not good enough."

"People won't accept me."

"I'm stupid, and I can't do anything right."

"I'm so ugly."

"God could never forgive me for what I did."

"I messed up, so God won't use me now."

"The divorce was all my fault."

Just a few words, in a little sentence, are all it takes. If we hear it enough, we begin to believe it. Believing it will lead to confessing it. That verbal declaration will bring us into agreement with the lie, which then has authority to move in that area of our life.

Even as I'm sitting in front of the computer writing this, I can sense the presence of the Holy Spirit moving on you. One of the wonderful gifts of the Spirit is discernment, which is clarity of mind and heart that moves on us as we open our hearts to Him.

If Jesus is the Christ, our Savior, and His truth will set us free, then why not ask Him to tell you the truth? He so desires to reveal Himself as the truth to us. New levels of clarity can come, no matter where we are in our walk with Him. I was in my 14th year of full-time pastoral ministry when the new clarity of this truth came to me.

Simply take that lie, the one you have heard for far too long, and ask Jesus if it's true. Quiet your spirit, and just ask Him: "Jesus, is it true that I'm not good enough?"

He will answer because He wants you to know the Truth; He's been waiting for you to ask. He loves you! He so desires for you to succeed and wants to right the wrongs and fill the emptiness with the words that should have been spoken over you, words that your teacher should have said. Words of approval you never heard from your earthly father. Let Jesus fill those chasms with His stamp of approval.

I can hear Him whispering into your spirit, "You are more than enough! You are My righteousness!" He says to you, "I accept you, and I will never leave you or forsake you!" He says to you, "I made you smart, witty and intelligent! I don't make ugly; you are beautifully and wonderfully made!" and, "Yes, I forgave you and forgot your sin as far as the east is from the west!"

Jesus wants you to know, "Your past in under My shed blood, and through My redemptive power, I will use you mightily!" To those who live with the pain of a loss or a broken home, He says, "It's not your fault, My child. I cried when you cried, and I will carry you through this. My heart is for you, not against you."

As you present each lie to Jesus, who is the Way, the

Truth and the Life, He will speak clearly, and that transparent work will expose the inroad of the enemy. Then repent for believing that lie, and cancel that contract in the name of Jesus!

It was Jesus who called you, healed you, freed you, qualified you and appointed you to pursue your mission. So go build that dream!

Building a Dream — Camp Nahshii

Research and development is very helpful when venturing into a massive project. Camp Nahshii was more than just another ministry project. I was driven by a vision to build a youth camp where no other had been built, to provide a safe haven where indigenous youth could be free to connect with their Creator and a place where they could find healing and salvation through Jesus. Yes, I had a dream, but I sure didn't want to reinvent the wheel.

Meeting after meeting, I wanted to get some advice from other camp directors in my area. They all gave me great help: information, statistics, do's and don'ts and their stories. But what I wanted to know the most was, "How did you get started?" "How did you start your camp?" and most important to me was, "How long did it take you before you provided your first year of camp?" The answers to this last question should have taken the wind out of my sails, and looking back, I sure think it would have if I had not already heard clearly from the Lord.

From one of these camp leaders I heard, "It took us eight years just to secure the property, then another five years before we started."

From another: "You should expect at least 10 years to get this up and running."

And another: "Are you ready for the great cost to build a camp? Having a camp located that remotely will not be cost-effective."

This theme of advice continued with each and every meeting. When each would give me his timeframe estimate, I would follow up with, "I'm sure it could take that long in most cases, but the Lord told me to build it and run it the first summer." You should have seen their faces. And I didn't blame them. This sounded completely nuts as it rolled off my tongue.

[4]To give prudence to the naive, to the youth knowledge and discretion, [5]a wise man will hear and increase in learning, and a man of understanding will acquire wise counsel, [6]to understand a proverb and a figure, the words of the wise and their riddles (Proverbs 1:4-6).

Acquiring wise counsel is simply that: wise. The key to finding wise counsel is finding someone who trusts the Word of the Lord as much as you do. Our mission never calls us to live the "Lone Ranger" approach or go "Rambo," chasing our dream with guns a-blazing.

[21]Folly is joy to him who lacks sense, but a man of understanding walks straight. [22]Without consultation, plans are frustrated, but with many counselors they

succeed. ²³*A man has joy in an apt answer, and how delightful is a timely word! (Proverbs 15:21-23).*

That "timely word" often comes from the counsel of others. I keep people in my life who are not intimidated by me and who will tell the truth, not from their experienced opinion, but from hearing the Lord speak. There are times when your greatest counsel is the history of how God came through in the past.

²³*Even though princes sit and talk against me, Your servant meditates on Your statutes.* ²⁴*Your testimonies also are my delight; they are my counselors (Psalm 119:23-24).*

When you are up against a mountain, sometimes you just need to be reminded of that last mountain God got you over, pulled you through or helped you remove. Your testimony may be the encouragement you need, and if you continually keep the presences of the Lord in your heart, you will not be shaken from your mission, your dream and your destiny.

⁷*I will bless the Lord who has counseled me; indeed, my mind instructs me in the night.* ⁸*I have set the Lord continually before me; because He is at my right hand, I will not be shaken (Psalm 16:7-8).*

The counsel from camp directors and pastors was sound, full of wisdom and information. According to this collective voice, we had a very long haul ahead of us. Or did we?

I had a vision to follow! A mandate to build this camp! And somehow, with the strength and provision of the

Lord, we were gonna do this thing. A local Native elder had offered me 40 acres of his land on which to build the camp, and I knew this was provision from God. I knew we just had to set our face like flint and get 'er done.

⁴The Lord God has given me the tongue of disciples, that I may know how to sustain the weary one with a word. He awakens me morning by morning, He awakens my ear to listen as a disciple. ⁵The Lord God has opened my ear; and I was not disobedient, nor did I turn back. ⁶I gave my back to those who strike me, and my cheeks to those who pluck out the beard; I did not cover my face from humiliation and spitting. ⁷For the Lord God helps me, therefore, I am not disgraced; therefore, **I have set my face like flint***, and I know that I will not be ashamed (Isaiah 50:4-7).*

Some said it would be way too far, too hard, too remote and definitely too expensive. Well, it is pretty far, it was very hard and it is expensive. But we did it, anyway, because these kids are worth it. Love will motivate you to larger steps of faith. Counsel is good, and seeking wisdom is necessary, but sometimes you just need to stay on course with the vision that God downloads into your heart. Remember the great things that God has done and know that He will come through again.

That spring after our lead trip to the property, we returned to the property with all we had. We were not a big team, but we were focused and driven to build a camp.

In our preparation, the Lord met our every need. We needed a portable sawmill, and He provided a new sawmill. We needed logging equipment, and He provided logging tools and equipment. We needed generators to power everything, and God provided those as well. This provision of Father God continued to repeat as we prayed and obeyed.

After the long and grueling adventure with the German raft, it took us several days to go the 150 miles to the property. We arrived in the evening and wasted no time getting started.

We had gone days without sleep, but there was no room on this land to pitch a tent, and tents were all we had. Working a section of ground until it was large enough to make a camp for this team took all night. It was 6 a.m. when we had cleared enough brush, trees and logs and leveled the ground so we could erect our tent city. By 8 a.m., we were finally climbing into our much-awaited homes for what would be some of the most appreciated sleep that we ever had. The next two months would be filled with long days of clearing land, moving brush, processing fallen trees and hand-carrying logs to the sawmill. We made our own lumber and started building the first project, an outhouse.

Looking back, we can see how the Spirit of the Lord gave us supernatural strength and energy to work those long hours, day after day, keeping the goal in view, while fighting off mosquitoes and bears.

We cleared enough land to host the campers, built a functional outdoor kitchen and constructed a traditional gathering area to house the services. It was a daunting task, but a task that we completed just in time to run our first of many summer camps!

That first summer, we were pleased to have 11 youth from three villages come, and we saw God bless us with great increase in campers in the summers that followed. After a few years, the numbers forced us to expand to two camps, and the influence continues to grow to this day. The Lord continued to bless, and our ministry now owns the 40 acres of land that this remote camp sits on.

Building this camp should have taken 10 years, and according to the world's standards, we certainly were not even close to being qualified enough for this job. It should have flopped. We should have failed.

But God *super* steps into our *natural* whenever we step out of our comfort zone and take leaps of faith in Him. When we activate our faith with a resounding "YES!" to the heavenly mission God gave to us, we engage a special anointing that is poured over that vision and strengthens us through it and to it.

Each summer, we are blessed with missionary work teams that travel far into the north to help take this dream to the next step. People just like us, people just like you. Does God only use the amazingly gifted? Does He prefer the overly talented? Is He more prone to anoint those with the most experience? Well, if any of that is true, then this camp should not exist, because we simply don't fit those requirements. Try to get this: It's not that God can't or won't use our giftedness, talent or experience. It's just that He doesn't require that of us.

What He does require is our obedience. Not simply saying yes because we know it's the right thing to do. But saying it because we are actually excited to see God's work done through us.

When He sees our love for His kids, heavenly approval is released on us to move that vision forward. And this anointed approval will far exceed any gift, talent or experience that we might be lacking. It's in this "lack" that the Father God likes to show up!

Stamp of Approval

We are all wired to want approval. We all need it. It's in our DNA to desire approval. We need it so that we have permission to get to the next level, chase after that dream and run freely in hot pursuit of our destiny.

Check this out: *The very God-vision that drives us in this mission comes packaged with His approval.* If our Heavenly Father has called you to a mission field, at any level of commitment, short-, mid- or long-term, then He must trust you with that calling. You see, you have His approval. You are highly favored, and with Christ, you CAN do ALL things!

You have His approval to do your amazing part of this kingdom work, to climb that massive mountain, to kill the giant and to do so knowing that the *Pro* of your *Vision* will supply the PROVISION.

Warriors of the Cross

Raising up legitimate missionaries of longevity is the

answer to this great need in His mission fields. This raising up and training up of warriors of the Cross will supernaturally take place as a direct result of our response to the GO! Our obedience will actually empower others to obey their call. As you and I persevere in this Great Commission, influenced by the Holy Spirit and *not* our feelings, many observers will be encouraged and follow suit.

¹Now after this the Lord appointed seventy others, and sent them in pairs ahead of Him to every city and place where He Himself was going to come. ²And He was saying to them, "The harvest is plentiful, but the laborers are few; therefore beseech the Lord of the harvest to send out laborers into His harvest. ³Go; behold, I send you out as lambs in the midst of wolves. ⁴Carry no money belt, no bag, no shoes; and greet no one on the way. ⁵Whatever house you enter, first say, 'Peace be to this house.' ⁶If a man of peace is there, your peace will rest on him; but if not, it will return to you. ⁷Stay in that house, eating and drinking what they give you; for the laborer is worthy of his wages. Do not keep moving from house to house. ⁸Whatever city you enter and they receive you, eat what is set before you; ⁹and heal those in it who are sick, and say to them, 'The kingdom of God has come near to you'" (Luke 10:1-9).

Let's take a closer look at these first nine verses of Chapter 10.

¹Now after this the Lord appointed seventy others, and sent them in pairs ahead of Him to every city and place where He Himself was going to come. ²And He was saying to them, "The harvest is plentiful, but the laborers are few; therefore beseech the Lord of the harvest to send out laborers into His harvest."

be·seech verb (used with object):
1. to implore urgently: They besought him to go at once
2. to beg eagerly for; solicit
3. to make urgent appeal

The Greek work for "beseech" in this verse is deomai (de'-o-mi), meaning:
1. to want, to desire, to ask, beg
2. to pray, make supplications

We have fields ready for harvest. And these fields are important to Jesus because they are His fields and His harvest. We need workers for these fields.

Ask the Lord to "send" out the laborers. The English word "send" is weaker than the original Greek word: "to thrust, to cast out, to evict and to eject" (*Strong's Concordance*). This was directed at the church, not the world.

We need to implore urgently. Beg eagerly. Beseech the Lord to send workers and laborers, missionaries to the fields — while looking in the mirror. Because we are the workers He desires to send to those fields!

QUALIFICATIONS

³Go; behold, I send you out as lambs in the midst of wolves.

Go! Prepared for battle. Predators don't simply lie down and surrender. Jesus exemplified a Lamb, a Shepherd and a Lion.

⁴Carry no money belt, no bag, no shoes; and greet no one on the way.

Don't worry about all the stuff! Prepare your heart, but don't worry about your duffle bag. This statement was not focused on the stuff or implying unpreparedness will be rewarded. This is all about trust. Don't let the lack of resources collected stop your travel. Trust in the one who owns those mission fields.

⁵Whatever house you enter, first say, "Peace be to this house." ⁶If a man of peace is there, your peace will rest on him; but if not, it will return to you.

Understand that not everyone will accept you and support you. But when they do, bless him and his house. It's not about you, it's about the lost. God didn't call you into the ministry to give you lots of friends. He called you to do a work. You're part of a bigger picture.

⁷Stay in that house, eating and drinking what they give you; for the laborer is worthy of his wages. Do not keep moving from house to house.

Don't move around, stay in one place. Once you find a door opened by the Lord, stay and become a blessing to them. Whatever happened to "stick-to-itiveness" and "longevity" in ministry? Don't move around. Build relationship, and stay until God actually moves you.

8Whatever city you enter and they receive you, eat what is set before you.

Eat what they eat! Honor the culture that you want to reach by enjoying their food. Be careful not to dishonor by putting personal preference ahead of principle. And remember: Real warriors of the Cross aren't picky, finicky or inflexible!

9and heal those in it who are sick, and say to them, "The kingdom of God has come near to you."

Bring healing to those who are there! Activate faith by walking in the gifts of the Holy Spirit. Tell them about the kingdom. Make "telling the story" a lifestyle. Don't simply give them Biblical information. Give them Holy Spirit impartations!

High and Dry — The Rest of the Story

What a beautiful sight! When we saw that boat coming downriver looking for us, we knew that short radio transmission had actually worked! I walked more than 100 yards in the shallow river to get close enough to yell out instructions. Jamie knew what she was doing and began to make large consistent wakes while we pushed, pulled, rocked and lifted this 24-foot monster. It was far too shallow for her to bring the other boat close enough for a tow, so "making waves" was the best way to help us out.

The waves help create life in the slow-moving part of the river, sending water to our shallow situation. After a few hours of teamwork, we were back to floating again.

Just needed to kick out all the gravel from the jet unit and fire up the 200hp motor. It was time to get back to the rest of my ministry team!

Sometimes, you just need to make waves to get a situation moving. You might need to rock the boat to get a boat out of a jam, to keep a vision from sitting still, to get moving forward. And sometimes you need a little disaster, right in the middle of your mission, even if it is self-inflicted. It helps to bring the team together in unity.

The challenges we encountered over the rest of this mission were no biggie. After that challenge, we knew we could get through anything together. Besides, we can do ALL things (even forgive our nutty leader) through Christ Jesus!

But in all these things we overwhelmingly conquer through Him who loved us (Romans 8:37).

I like that: "Overwhelmingly conquer!" With the confidence that comes from our Heavenly Father, who gave us this mission, we are able to declare:

Mission Accomplished.

Author's Thanks

Throughout the writing process there have been those who greatly invested in this project. From those who helped finance the publishing to those who helped impart the passion, many are deserving of my thanks.

Let me start with thanking Ken Horn, editor of the *Pentecostal Evangel.* His feedback to my "Cross-Cultural Ministry" workshop back in 2008 planted the seed in my heart to write on this subject. His heartfelt foreword to this book is personally encouraging and professionally appreciated.

Thanks to Jeremiah Niemuth, U.S. Missionary and Pastor of Fort Yukon Assembly. His countless hours executing the pre-edit of the manuscript and the time he invested in fixing my sorry attempt at the English language is a real blessing to me.

Thanks to all those who showed their belief in this writing by contributing their endorsements. Your experience and wonderful feedback were overwhelmingly encouraging.

Thanks to my faithful staff. Their endless support and encouragement kept my head and heart focused. Their willingness to run with the ball while I was buried in deadlines was a welcomed blessing.

Thanks to my loving and supportive parents. I could always count on their excitement about the book, even when the end looked far off. The consistent support Dad and Mom invested over the years positioned me to set goals and standards high.

SPECIAL THANKS to my family. Their support and personal sacrifice was a great investment in this book. Thanks is owed to my three kids: They endured my many hours glued to the monitor and all too often ignoring them during this project. I appreciate them with sincere endearment. Jovanna, Cody and Austin inspire me more than they will ever know! Much thanks to my best friend and personal prayer warrior, Yolanda. Her sleepless nights of intercession over me and our family were inspiring. She believed in me, even in those times when I struggled with believing in myself. Her input was and continues to be priceless to my success.

Acknowledgements

I would like to thank Jane Allen Petrick, project manager and editor, for the vision, hard work, prayer and faith she put into this book to make it a reality. Her untiring resolve pushed this project forward and turned it into a stunning victory. Thank you for your great fortitude and diligence.

Deep thanks to our incredible editor in chief, Michelle Cuthrell, and executive editor, Jen Genovesi, for all the amazing work they do. I would also like to thank our invaluable proofreader, Melody Davis, for the focus and energy she has put into perfecting our words.

Lastly, I want to extend our gratitude to the creative and very talented Jenny Randle, who designed the beautiful cover for *Mission Accomplished: The Secrets of Successful Missions.*

Daren Lindley
President and CEO
Good Book Publishing

ABOUT THE AUTHOR

Ron Pratt grew up in a minister's home in Southern California. His first personal encounter with Jesus took place at the age of 8.

It was during that salvation experience Ron knew he had heard the call to a life of ministry.

Pastor Pratt started his ministry to young people in Modesto, California, in 1983. Then, in 1998, along with his wife, Yolanda, two children and one on the way, he moved north to North Pole, Alaska. There he accepted a position that would greatly expand his ministry calling by starting the first Master's Commission discipleship school in the state.

Ron's intensity and passion for the lost is displayed in his commitment to others. Discipleship is much more than a buzzword to Ron Pratt. It is the foundation of his focus, purpose and destiny.

A gifted communicator and preacher, Ron has ministered throughout the United States, Mexico and Europe. His vision and creativity to reach hurting people is contagious. Restoring cultural protocols and showing honor are some of the effective ministry methods that he not only practices, but also teaches to others. When attending one of his workshops or seminars, it becomes obvious that he is purpose-driven to help others become who they are in Christ. He believes the body of Christ should laugh more and enjoy the road to their destiny. His humorous approach to ministry is anointed, as well as full of impartation and revelatory nuggets of truth.

Bringing healing and hope to the remote communities and villages of Alaska is a mandate Ron continues to pursue with intense love and compassion for the people of the North.

As president and founder of This Generation Ministries, Ron continues to lead the TGM vision and mandate to reach the lost of Alaska, then train and release them to carry forth the Gospel.

You can follow Ron on Twitter @Ron_Pratt.

For more information on Ron Pratt
and This Generation Ministries:

Mailing Address:
550 Beaver Blvd,
North Pole, Alaska 99705

Phone Number:
907.978.6821 or 907.978.5822

E-mail Address:
RonPrattAlaska@gmail.com

To order more copies of this book, visit:
Book Web site: www.RonPrattAlaska.com

To learn more about This Generation Ministries, visit:
TGM Web site: www.tgmalaska.com

You can follow Ron on Twitter @Ron_Pratt

GOOD BOOK
PUBLISHING

www.goodbookpublishing.com